STRATEGIC ATTACK

Air Force Doctrine Document 3-70
12 June 2007

Interim Change 2 (Last Review), 1 November 2011

This document complements related discussion found in Joint Publication 3-0, *Joint Operations*.

SUMMARY OF CHANGES

The Air Force Doctrine Working Group has reviewed this document and recommended that it remains valid and will again be reviewed no later than September 2012. AFDD numbering has also been changed to correspond with the joint doctrine publication numbering architecture. AFDD titles and content remain unchanged until updated in the next full revision. A margin bar indicates newly revised material.

Old Number	New Number	Title
AFDD 2-1	changed to AFDD 3-1	*Air Warfare*
AFDD 2-1.1	changed to AFDD 3-01	Counterair Operations
AFDD 2-1.2	changed to AFDD 3-70	Strategic Attack
AFDD 2-1.3	changed to AFDD 3-03	Counterland Operations
AFDD 2-1.4	changed to AFDD 3-04	Countersea Operations
AFDD 2-1.6	changed to AFDD 3-50	Personnel Recovery Operations
AFDD 2-1.7	changed to AFDD 3-52	Airspace Control
AFDD 2-1.8	changed to AFDD 3-40	Counter-CBRN
AFDD 2-1.9	changed to AFDD 3-60	Targeting
AFDD 2-10	changed to AFDD 3-27	Homeland Operations
AFDD 2-12	changed to AFDD 3-72	Nuclear Operations
AFDD 2-2	changed to AFDD 3-14	Space Operations
AFDD 2-2.1	changed to AFDD 3-14.1	Counterspace Operations
AFDD 2-3	changed to AFDD 3-24	Irregular Warfare
AFDD 2-3.1	changed to AFDD 3-22	Foreign Internal Defense
AFDD 2-4	changed to AFDD 4-0	Combat Support
AFDD 2-4.1	changed to AFDD 3-10	Force Protection
AFDD 2-4.2	changed to AFDD 4-02	Health Services
AFDD 2-4.4	changed to AFDD 4-11	Bases, Infrastructure... [Rescinded]
AFDD 2-4.5	changed to AFDD 1-04	Legal Support
AFDD 2-5	changed to AFDD 3-13	Information Operations
AFDD 2-5.1	changed to AFDD 3-13.1	Electronic Warfare
AFDD 2-5.3	changed to AFDD 3-61	Public Affairs Operations
AFDD 2-6	changed to AFDD 3-17	Air Mobility Operations
AFDD 2-7	changed to AFDD 3-05	Special Operations
AFDD 2-8	changed to AFDD 6-0	Command and Control
AFDD 2-9	changed to AFDD 2-0	ISR Operations
AFDD 2-9.1	changed to AFDD 3-59	Weather Operations

Supersedes: AFDD 2-1.2, 30 September 2003
OPR: LeMay Center/DD
Certified by: LeMay Center/DD
Pages: 58
Accessibility: Available on the e-publishing website at www.e-publishing.af.mil for
            downloading
Releasability: There are no releasability restrictions on this publication
Approved by: LeMay Center/CC, Maj Gen Thomas K. Andersen, USAF
            Commander, LeMay Center for Doctrine Development and Education

FOREWORD

War is one of mankind's most complex endeavors. Destroying or incapacitating enemy military forces and attriting them into ineffectiveness is one means, but not the only means, of achieving warfare's objectives. Airmen have always envisioned going directly to the heart of an enemy. Modern air, space, and cyberspace power has come a long way toward realizing this vision. The combination of advanced systems with stealth and precision has made airpower a force to be reckoned with. Commanders now have the capability to directly affect an adversary's strategic center of gravity, helping to accelerate achievement of US national objectives.

Strategic attack is offensive action specifically selected to achieve national strategic objectives. These attacks seek to weaken the adversary's ability or will to engage in conflict, and may achieve strategic objectives without necessarily having to achieve operational objectives as a precondition. Strategic attack involves the systematic application of force against enemy systems and their centers of gravity, thereby producing the greatest effect for the least cost in blood and treasure. Vital systems to be affected may include leadership, critical processes, popular will and perception, and fielded forces. Strategic attack provides an effective capability that may drive an early end to conflict or achieve objectives more directly or efficiently than other applications of military power.

Air, space, and cyberspace power has inherent, unique advantages in conducting strategic attack, with the distinct aim is producing effects well beyond the immediate tactical and operational effort expended and of directly contributing to achieving strategic, war-winning effects and objectives.

Air Force Doctrine Document 2-1.2, *Strategic Attack*, is doctrine for understanding, planning, and executing this crucial function across the range of military operations. Air Force personnel need to be able to articulate the rationale for strategic attack as an essential and valuable warfighting option for the combatant commander. More importantly, Air Force personnel must understand how strategic attack can help fulfill or enhance our national security and military strategies as a tool for defeating our nation's adversaries.

ALLEN G. PECK
Major General, USAF
Commander, Headquarters
Air Force Doctrine Center

TABLE OF CONTENTS

INTRODUCTION

PURPOSE

This Air Force doctrine document (AFDD) establishes doctrinal guidance for the United States Air Force on strategic attack. It articulates fundamental Air Force principles for the application of combat force and provides commanders operational guidance on the employment and integration of Air Force resources to achieve desired objectives.

APPLICATION

This AFDD applies to the Total Force: all Air Force military and civilian personnel, including regular, Air Force Reserve, and Air National Guard units and members. Unless specifically stated otherwise, Air Force doctrine applies to the full range of military operations.

The doctrine in this document is authoritative, but not directive. Therefore, commanders need to consider the contents of this AFDD and the particular situation when accomplishing their missions. Airmen should read it, discuss it, and practice it.

SCOPE

This doctrine provides guidance for planning and conducting strategic attack in support of our national security and combatant/joint force commander objectives.

COMAFFOR / JFACC / CFACC
A note on terminology

One of the cornerstones of Air Force doctrine is that the US Air Force prefers—and in fact, plans and trains—to employ through a commander of Air Force forces (COMAFFOR) who is also dual-hatted as a joint force air, space, and cyberspace component commander (JFACC).

To simplify the use of nomenclature, Air Force doctrine documents will assume the COMAFFOR is dual-hatted as the JFACC unless specifically stated otherwise. The term "COMAFFOR" refers to the Air Force Service component commander while the term "JFACC" refers to the joint component-level operational commander.

While both joint and Air Force doctrine state that one individual will normally be dual-hatted as COMAFFOR and JFACC, the two responsibilities are different, and should be executed through different staffs.

Normally, the COMAFFOR function executes operational control/ administrative control of assigned and attached Air Force forces through a Service A-staff while the JFACC function executes tactical control of joint air and space component forces through an air and space operations center (AOC).

When multinational operations are involved, the JFACC becomes a combined force air, space, and cyberspace component commander (CFACC). Likewise, the air and space operations center, though commonly referred to as an AOC in joint or combined operations, is correctly known as a joint AOC (JAOC) or combined AOC (CAOC).

Since nearly every operation the US conducts will involve international partners, this publication uses the terms CFACC and CAOC throughout to emphasize the doctrine's applicability to multi-national operations.

FOUNDATIONAL DOCTRINE STATEMENTS

Foundational doctrine statements are the basic principles and beliefs upon which AFDDs are built. Other information in the AFDD expands on or supports these statements.

✪ Strategic attack (SA) is offensive action that is specifically selected to achieve national strategic objectives. These attacks seek to weaken the adversary's ability or will to engage in conflict, and may achieve strategic objectives without necessarily having to achieve operational objectives as a precondition. (Page 2)

✪ SA seizes upon the unique capability of air, space, and cyberspace power to achieve objectives by striking at the heart of the enemy, disrupting critical leadership functions, infrastructure, and strategy, while at the same time avoiding a sequential fight through layers of forces. (Page 4)

✪ SA achieves objectives through indirect effects. (Page 7)

✪ SA can play a crucial role in coercing an enemy into adopting a desired course of action. (Page 10)

✪ Unity of effort is key to the success of SA operations and can only be achieved through command and control arrangements that ensure unity of command. (Page 13)

✪ When air operations constitute the bulk of SA capability, the joint force commander (JFC) will normally task the joint force air and space component commander, as a supported commander, to conduct such operations. (Page 15)

✪ The commander, Air Force forces should provide the JFC with SA options early in the planning process. (Page 16)

✪ Effective use of SA requires clear, attainable, relevant, and decisive objectives. It also requires clear definition of the commander's criteria for the operation's overall success—a logical and achievable end state. (Page 18)

✪ SA is normally most effective when employed using parallel operations. (Page 30)

CHAPTER ONE

FUNDAMENTALS OF STRATEGIC ATTACK

DEFINING ROLE FOR AIR, SPACE, AND CYBERSPACE POWER

Department of Defense (DOD) Directive 5100.1, *Functions of the DOD and Its Major Components*, states that the Air Force is specifically directed to "organize, train, equip, and provide forces for...strategic air and missile warfare." Formerly, strategic attack (SA) was defined in terms of nuclear delivery systems or weapons. This is no longer true. SA is not defined in terms of weapons or delivery systems used—their type, range, speed, or destructiveness—but by its effective contribution to achieving strategic objectives.

Historical Strategic Attack Examples

✪ Alexander the Great defeated the Persians at Issus (331 B.C.) by leading a cavalry assault at King Darius himself (a center of gravity), which removed Darius from the battlefield and resulted in the Persian Army leaving their positions in full rout.

✪ Charles Martel's Frankish infantry at Tours in 732 isolated Muslim Emir Abd-er-Rahman and "pierced him through with many spears, so that he died; then all the [Muslim] host fled before the enemy"... thus saving Western Europe from Muslim domination.

✪ Allied bomber crews and commando teams destroyed the German heavy water program—and Hitler's hope for an atomic bomb with it—during World War II.

✪ Allied submarines destroyed Japanese merchant shipping in the Pacific during World War II, consciously avoiding engagement with Japanese naval forces while denying Japan crucial war-sustaining resources.

✪ North Atlantic Treaty Organization (NATO) SA operations coerced Yugoslav leader Slobodan Milosevic to submit to NATO demands (1999).

—Various Sources

Advances in information technology, precision weaponry, tactics, and warfighting doctrine have made SA an even more capable tool, giving airpower the potential to achieve decisive effects more directly without the need to engage enemy fielded forces first. Operation DESERT STORM proved the efficacy of SA and Operations DELIBERATE FORCE (ODF), ALLIED FORCE (OAF), ENDURING FREEDOM (OEF), and IRAQI FREEDOM (OIF) further refined it. In these operations, air assets conducting SA have often proven able to deny the enemy access to critical resources and infrastructure, defeat enemy strategies, and decisively influence enemy decisions to end hostilities on terms favorable to US interests. In addition to its ability to destroy enemy surface forces and support friendly surface forces, today's Air Force provides joint force commanders with enormous lethal and non-lethal capabilities that can contribute **directly** to the achievement of strategic objectives.

Properly implemented, SA achieves disproportionate results. It allows commanders to literally strike at the enemy's heart and thus shape a conflict in ways favorable to the US. This publication examines what SA is and how to properly plan, execute, assess, and adapt it.

DEFINITION

SA is offensive action specifically selected to achieve national strategic objectives. These attacks seek to weaken the adversary's ability or will to engage in conflict, and may achieve strategic objectives without necessarily having to achieve operational objectives as a precondition.

SA is an approach to war focused on the adversary's overall system and the most effective way to target or influence that system. It examines the full spectrum of that system: Political, military, economic, social, infrastructure, and information in the context of stated national security objectives. SA involves the combination of effects that most effectively and efficiently achieves those objectives at the strategic level. In the Air Force context, SA is a discrete set of military operations aimed at achieving those strategic objectives. Air, space, and cyberspace power offers the quickest and most direct means to conduct those operations.

SA involves the systematic application of lethal and/or non-lethal capabilities against an enemy's strategic centers of gravity (COGs), to undermine the enemy's will and ability to threaten our national security interests. Strategic centers of gravity may include: Leadership; operational processes such as communications, electrical, petroleum etc; infrastructure such as railroads and bridges; popular will and perception; and fielded forces.

The civilian population and individual civilians shall enjoy general protection against dangers arising from military operations....The civilian population as such, as well as individual civilians, shall not be the object of attack.

—Geneva Additional Protocol I, Article 51

<u>Note</u>: Although the US is not a party to Protocol 1, the US considers many of the Protocol 1 provisions, including this one, to be either legally binding as customary international law or acceptable practice, though not legally binding. It should also be noted that Geneva Convention IV and Hague Convention IV, both of which the US has signed, provide various protections for civilians and civilian populations, and limit the right of belligerents to adopt means of injuring the enemy.

SA includes analysis, planning, targeting, command and control (C2), execution, and assessment in combination to support achievement of strategic objectives. An analysis of the definition clarifies SA:

- ✪ "Strategic" refers to the highest level of an enemy system that, if affected, will contribute most directly to the achievement of our national security objectives. It does not mean nuclear, although in some instances the weapon most appropriate for a particular set of circumstances may be nuclear. (System: A regularly interacting or interdependent group of items forming a unified whole... [Merriam-Webster Online Dictionary])

- ✪ "Attack" entails offensive, proactive action. It implies aggressive operations conducted against an enemy state, non-state, or other organization and may be used preemptively and without regard to the enemy military force. Attacks may employ lethal or nonlethal means, from conventional destructive weapons to forms of cyber power such as network attack.

- ✪ The aim of SA is to contribute directly to the achievement of national security objectives by generating effects that significantly influence centers of gravity. SA operations are essentially effects-based and should be planned, executed, and assessed as part of a seamless, adaptive whole, starting with the desired outcome and working backwards to determine the required actions/effects. It is focused on the objectives achieved rather than the platforms, weapons, or methods used.

- ✪ SA is oriented on the adversary's system, changing it to conform to our national objectives. SA accomplishes this change by affecting (positively or negatively) the COGs in the enemy (not just military) system that will force the overall system to change as desired in the shortest possible period of time. COGs are the leverage points in the system that, when affected, create significantly more change than would be achieved by affecting parts of the system that are not centers of gravity. COGs can be physical things like leaders, key production, structures, people, or organizations. Affecting COGs will yield results disproportionate to the effort expended, that is, they will provide the highest payoff (enemy system change) for the least cost (lives, resources, time, etc).

- ✪ A center of gravity is defined in joint doctrine as the source of power that provides moral strength, freedom of action, or will to act. In the context of SA against enemy systems, COGs are focal points that hold a system or structure together and draw power from a variety of sources and provide purpose and direction to that system. In practical terms, COGs have critical requirements, some of which may be vulnerable to attack – critical vulnerabilities. These critical vulnerabilities may yield decisive points: geographic places, specific key events, critical factors, or functions that, when acted upon, allow commanders to gain a marked advantage over an adversary or contribute materially to creating a desired effect. Affecting these decisive points should exploit a COG's critical vulnerabilities in a manner that creates desired effects against the COG itself. SA may often be the function of choice for exploiting adversary decisive points.

✪ SA affects conflict-sustaining resources. While it may often be difficult to directly target an adversary's will, we can often target the means the adversary employs to conduct or continue the conflict. Modern high-technology warfare is resource intensive; the support necessary to sustain it provides many lucrative targets which, when attacked, speeds enemy collapse and removes options. This is true across the range of military operations and not just for modern, high-technology combat. The target sets may change, but the principle remains the same.

✪ SA affects the enemy's strategy. Sun Tzu said the best policy in war is to defeat the enemy's strategy; this requires we hold at risk what the enemy holds dear or deny them the ability to obtain what they seek. While other forms of military or national power can also deny the enemy strategic choices, SA can often do so more effectively and efficiently.

BASIC CHARACTERISTICS

SA seizes upon the unique capability of air, space, and cyberspace to achieve objectives by striking at the heart of the enemy, disrupting critical leadership functions, infrastructure, and strategy, while at the same time avoiding a sequential fight through layers of forces.

Unless the enemy's military forces are deemed to be a strategic COG, they are not useful as SA targets. In fact, the goal of SA operations is to bypass the fielded forces to the maximum extent possible. A way to illustrate this concept is to think of the military as a tool being used by a nation or organization to enforce or force its will. It very often makes more sense to attack the person, nation, or organization using the tool rather than the tool itself. SA's goal is to exert influence on the decision-maker rather than the tool being used by the decision-maker.

Next, SA conducted against an enemy system in a deliberate, systematic way generates strategic-level effects without first having to fight the enemy's fielded forces. SA seeks to prevent an enemy from achieving goals (reactive) or enabling us to achieve our goals (proactive). By affecting strategic-level COGs, the results should be greater than those generated by a similar effort against peripheral systems or targets.

SA can also act on the psychology of the enemy leadership by changing the political climate or denying options or choices. These attacks could indirectly affect the adversary's will to fight.

> *During the combined bomber offensive (CBO) in Europe in World War II, Allied air attacks against the German rail and inland waterway systems fatally disrupted the German economy. Even though the productive capacity of individual factories increased through most of 1944, the disruption of transportation nearly immobilized the economy as a whole, almost stripped Germany of electrical power (due to disruption of coal shipments), and greatly hampered the movement of Germany's armies. These efforts might have ended the war in Europe by themselves had Germany's resistance in the field not been collapsing simultaneously.*

> *"The attack on transportation was the decisive blow that completely disorganized the German economy. It reduced war production in all categories and made it difficult to move what was produced to the front. The attack also limited the tactical mobility of the German army."*
>
> **— United States Strategic Bombing Survey Summary Report (European War)**

STRATEGIC ATTACK AND WARFIGHTING STRATEGY

SA represents one key element of a unified national approach to handling a conflict and should not be employed in isolation. A sound, unified approach will comprise diplomatic, informational, military, and economic activities orchestrated carefully to achieve national security objectives. It is most effectively used in a manner that complements and is complemented by other operations. For example, action against an enemy's forces may expose critical targets and increase their consumption of war-sustaining resources. Such operations may also be necessary to enable SA, as the defeat of the Luftwaffe through offensive counterair operations did during World War II. Certain coercive applications of SA simply may not work in the absence of complementary diplomatic, political, or economic actions.

Regardless of these considerations, the United States can pursue a comprehensive strategy designed to place maximum stress on the enemy system (nation or terrorist organization). The process of developing this strategy should start with the desired end state and then be worked backwards from big to little, strategic to tactical. The enemy should be analyzed as a system and an effects-based approach used to determine required effects and actions. Striking an enemy system's COGs should be accomplished as quickly and from as many directions and sources as possible, in order to place overwhelming strain on the system.

Victory in any conflict requires some mechanism for changing the enemy's behavior. Behavior can be influenced by affecting the enemy's capability to fight or by influencing his will to fight; most situations will involve aspects of both. There are several mechanisms that can be used to implement a coercive strategy (see Chapter 4).

OBJECTIVES AND EFFECTS

Centuries of surface warfare have conditioned leaders of world powers to raise armies and navies, the primary attributes of which are mobility, armor, firepower, depth, and sustained presence in foreign lands. These attributes are necessary to withstand force-on-force engagements until strategic breakthrough can be attained. Military force is one instrument of national power; bypassing it altogether or simultaneously attacking other instruments of national power or centers of gravity may result in a change of an adversary's ability or will to fight.

Strategic Objectives

Ends, not means, drive the SA effort. Successful SA requires clear and attainable objectives. Objectives and desired end states should be clearly understood by planners and commanders orchestrating the SA effort and should be tied to the SAs themselves by a clear, logical mechanism of cause and effect. SA operations are designed to produce political, military, economic, social, infrastructure, cyber, and information effects that contribute directly to achieving the strategic objectives of the joint force commander (JFC) and higher authorities. The senior commander and national leaders should also weigh SA operations against potential unintended effects, since attacking certain COGs could have undesired impacts on populations and neighboring countries. Strategic objectives, like those at all levels, should be measurable. Commanders and national leaders should know when those objectives are achieved.

Strategic Effects

Effects-Based Approach

"Effects-based" describes the operations that are planned, executed, assessed and adapted to influence or change systems or capabilities in order to achieve desired outcomes. Effective operations should be part of a coherent plan that logically ties all actions to the achievement of the desired end state.

NOTE: For a full discussion of the effects-based approach see AFDD 2, *Operations and Organization*.

SA seeks to achieve the greatest effect for the least cost in lives and resources by systematically applying force to COGs within the pertinent systems. Systematic application of force should not be confused with sequential application, but instead refers to a systematic approach to planning and executing attacks to achieve desired effects. System change that drives enemy compliance is the goal of SA. This system change will most effectively be achieved by applying force through parallel operations where the targeted systems are struck in a compressed timeframe. This type of attack has the highest probability of pushing a system beyond its ability to react or adapt.

Attempting to change the system through attacks on its periphery will not be as effective as overwhelming system-wide parallel attack.

SA achieves objectives through indirect effects. SA, even more than other forms of attack, is concerned with higher-level indirect effects. Direct effects are the results of actions with no intervening causal mechanism between act and outcome. Direct effects trigger additional outcomes—intermediate effects or mechanisms that produce higher-order outcomes or results. From the commander, Air Force forces' (COMAFFOR's) perspective, individual missions or sorties are actions that cause higher-order direct effects, which in turn cause indirect effects. An example might be the action of an aircraft dropping weapons, resulting in the direct effect of destroying a bridge span. This in turn leads to the indirect effects of impeding movement of enemy forces and perhaps, in terms of SA, by severing fiber-optic cables running under the bridge span, forcing the adversary to use alternate forms of communication. It may seem that indirect effects will take longer to be realized but in fact the end results will often occur sooner than if the operation begins at the periphery and moves to the heart.

The intended and desired indirect effects of SA may, however, coincide with unintended and undesired effects if there are gaps in our understanding of the operational environment. Destruction of a bridge span, for example, could also result in the unintended disruption of electrical power and telephone communications to a nearby community if we were unaware that these utilities were attached to the bridge. This could cause hardship in that community and erode any popular support that might have existed prior to the event. Commanders and planners must appreciate that unpredictable third-party actions, unintended consequences of friendly operations, subordinate initiative and creativity, and the fog and friction of conflict will contribute to an uncertain operational environment. (Joint Publication 5.0, *Joint Operations Planning*)

SA can generate all types of effects, including direct, indirect, physical, behavioral, or psychological, and may occur sequentially or in parallel, cascading or cumulative. The effects generally will occur as a result of how operations are conducted—usually parallel operations will result in parallel effects which put the most stress on a system and are most likely to result in permanent system change. Sequential operations generally yield sequential effects. Also, the type of system being attacked, the action taken against it, the number of nodes struck and the amount of time used to carry out the attacks will affect whether effects are cascading—sudden, catastrophic changes in system states that often affect surrounding related systems—or cumulative—building sequentially in small amounts toward system change. The more compressed the attack across a wide spectrum of the system, the more likely cascading effects are to occur.

Effects occur at all levels of operations. The relationships of SA and the traditional (or customary) approach to warfare are illustrated in Figure 1.1. The effects of SA should be felt at the strategic level and cascade down to the operational and tactical levels. Effects upon fielded forces will generally be a byproduct of achieving broader strategic objectives. For example, the British retaliatory bombing of Berlin during the Battle of Britain shocked Nazi leadership, provoking a decisive change in campaign focus. German attacks that had been distributed across southern Britain (and were sorely taxing Royal Air Force [RAF] Fighter Command) now concentrated on London, greatly facilitating defense efforts, relieving pressure on the beleaguered RAF, and ultimately turning the tide of the campaign in Britain's favor. The significant effect of the Berlin raid, although "indirect" from an effects-based perspective, was achieved directly upon Hitler and Goering. Subsequent effects cascaded down to the German Luftwaffe and the RAF at the operational and tactical levels.

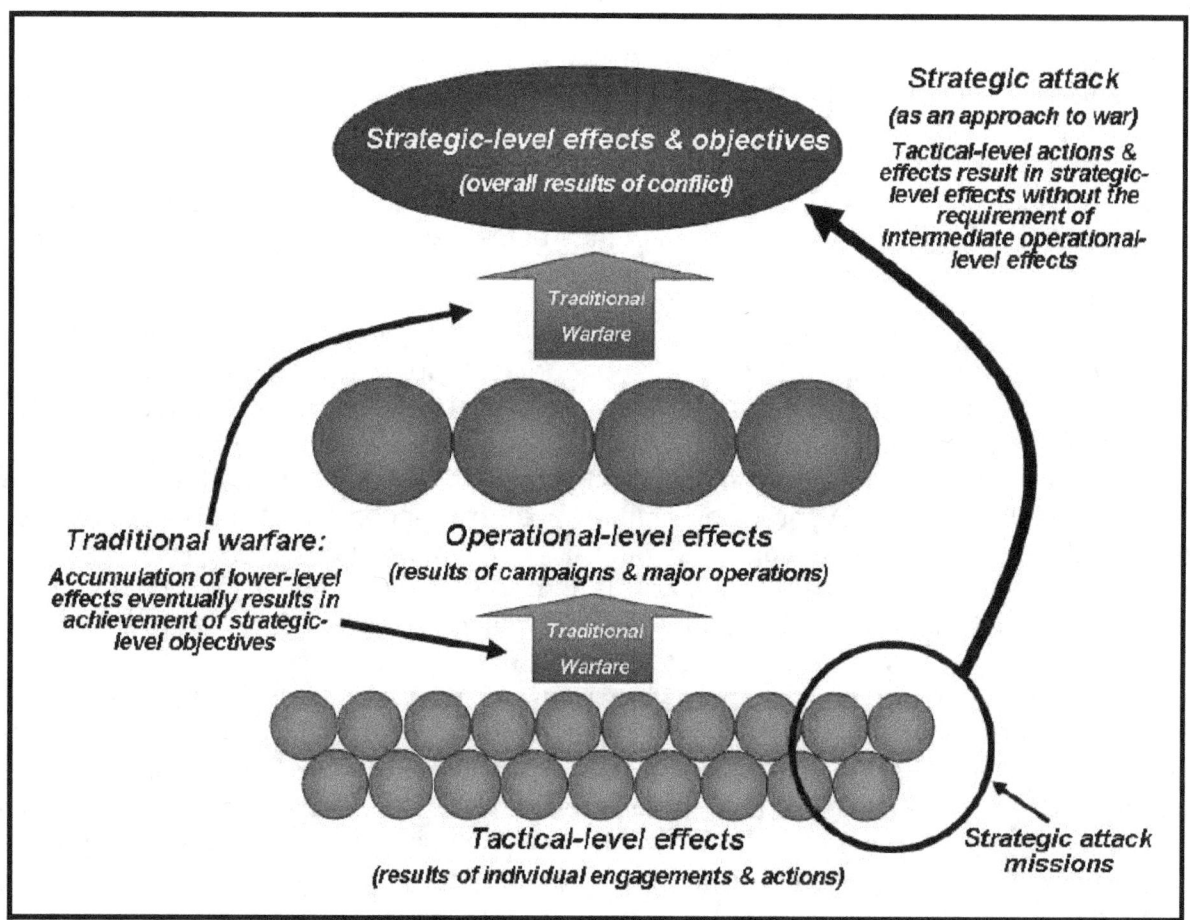

Figure 1.1. Strategic Attack and the Levels of War

Systemic Effects

Every party to a conflict, whether a modern nation-state or terrorist organization, is a complex, adaptive system. Every system has elements critical to its functioning: key strengths and sources of power. Some aspects or elements of every system are vulnerable to attack or influence. The key to understanding systemic effects is understanding how these two are related: what the system's critical vulnerabilities are. Each system has a leadership or governing function (e.g., Osama Bin Laden), some adaptable plan or strategy, some means of carrying out its strategy (armed forces or terrorist cadres), and key infrastructure supporting the system and allowing it to act on its strategy (communications, warfighting resources). SA seeks to incapacitate one or more of these key functions, either by affecting the functions themselves (attacks against leadership, for instance), or by affecting the linkages between them (as in severing the leadership's means of communication with its control mechanisms). Strategic attack may also undermine the elements providing support to these functions (for example, propaganda and internal security as they support leadership). Since components of complex systems are interrelated, affecting the appropriate linkages and nodes in one part of a system can cause cascading changes or failures throughout the system as a whole. Further, the disturbances that cause these changes can often be very small. Such efficiency is the soul of SA: finding those key relationships within systems where small inputs will yield desirable system-wide changes.

It is not possible to predict exactly what level of stress will cause a system to fail or change its behavior; that level may vary from day to day, even moment to moment. However, systems stressed with sufficient intensity and rapidity can suffer effects much like shock in the human body—relative inaction coupled with very low system energy levels. Shock is achieved when stress is induced faster than a system is able to adapt to it. Parallel attack may be the best means of inducing such shock: striking multiple targets across a system to induce system-wide stress while also striking critical nodes or vulnerabilities chosen to maximize dislocation effects within the system. This may hold the best prospect of causing cascading system-wide changes in behavior. SA is the critical method to create these effects and may be most efficient when conducted through parallel attack.

Decisive Effects

SA offers commanders many options for winning conflicts outright or for shaping them in decisive ways. It supports or underpins a variety of potential strategies.

Attacks on leadership can often provide significant strategic leverage. Attacks against Iraqi leader Saddam Hussein, his inner circle, and his key security infrastructure during OIF effectively decapitated the Iraqi military, opening the door for a swifter counterforce operation against the Republican Guard. Attacks against al Qaeda terrorist leaders in Afghanistan and Yemen are further examples of the successful removal of enemy leadership. Leadership can be affected in a variety of ways from removal to undermining popular support to isolation. Due to SA during DESERT STORM, Saddam Hussein was not removed but was forced to take protective measures that effectively reduced his command and control capability.

SA can be a very flexible tool effective across the range of military operations. Strikes against al Qaeda leadership took place during the major operations phase in Afghanistan, but those in Yemen were done outside the context of major operations, as part of the broader Global War on Terror. Cyberspace operations such as network attacks against terror systems across the globe are another example. This is an important insight: modern SA capabilities can create discrete, precise effects on short notice directly from the continental United States (CONUS). SA can be conducted across the range of military operations, as the strategic context warrants.

SA can deny an enemy the means and resources it requires to continue a conflict. Allied air attacks against the German transportation and oil industries eventually crippled German war production and significantly reduced Germany's intertheater mobility, which in turn significantly degraded the Wehrmacht's ability to maneuver and fight. Many potential adversaries today do not produce their own weapons, complicating interdiction or destruction of warfighting means. In many cases, cyber power can be used to deny an enemy access to financial and informational resources it needs to operate effectively. Such operations were used successfully against the Yugoslav regime during OAF.

SA can deny an enemy strategic options or choices. One example is the elimination or disruption of enemy weapons of mass destruction (WMD) programs. In World War II, British and Norwegian commandos successfully carried out raids against a Nazi heavy water production plant in Norway. This SA denied the Germans a critical capability in developing their version of the atomic bomb. It was also an important element of US and coalition strategy during and after Operation DESERT STORM, as a combination of coalition air strikes and UN inspections sought to deny the Iraqi regime access to WMD.

SA can also defeat an enemy strategy that is "in play." During Operation DESERT STORM, SAs against Iraqi surface-to-surface missile system (SCUD) missiles combined with strategic defensive measures and deft political initiatives countered Saddam Hussein's intended strategy of breaking the US-led coalition by dragging Israel into the war. SCUD suppression efforts achieved the politically vital effect of dissuading Israeli retaliation and thus were critical to maintaining the coalition, despite the fact that few "hard kills" were achieved.

SA can play an important part in a strategy designed to break apart an enemy warfighting coalition or use its system of alliances against it. It can also be used to help hold together a friendly coalition. In 1943, Allied air attacks against Rome played a crucial role both in driving Italian dictator Benito Mussolini from power and in coercing Mussolini's successor to surrender. Rome had been "off-limits" to Allied bombing until July 1943, when Allied leaders made a conscious decision to twice bomb a rail yard near the center of the city in order to induce psychological shock that would help drive Italy from the war. The effort was successful and deprived the Axis one of its important component states. During OAF, NATO's deliberate increase in the intensity of SA operations against Yugoslavia coupled with its diplomatic initiatives helped convince Russia of NATO's resolve. Russia then used its influence to pressure Yugoslav president Milosevic to accede to NATO's demands.

SA can play a crucial role in coercing an enemy into adopting a desired course of action. Often, this involves accession to demands other than simple capitulation, although that may be among the desired objectives. In successful instances, SA is most often coupled with complementary diplomatic and information initiatives. In December 1972, the US bombing campaign along with Operation POCKET MONEY (the mining of Haiphong harbor and other North Vietnamese ports) combined effectively with diplomatic pressure to coerce the North Vietnamese leadership to the come to the Paris peace talks. US-led efforts to defeat the North Vietnamese Easter Offensive in 1972 culminated in Operation LINEBACKER I (largely an aerial interdiction effort), which stopped North Vietnamese action in the field. This created the context for diplomatic initiatives, which made good progress until after the US November elections. Post-election North Vietnamese diplomatic retrenchment was answered with Operation LINEBACKER II's SAs against COGs in Hanoi and Haiphong harbor, which effectively coerced the North Vietnamese into signing a peace accord amenable to the US. As previously mentioned, coercion efforts also drove Milosevic to withdraw his troops from Kosovo and sign the peace agreement ending OAF.

> *In our victory over Japan, airpower was unquestionably decisive. That the planned invasion of the Japanese Home islands was unnecessary is clear evidence that airpower has evolved into a force in war co-equal with land and sea power, decisive in its own right and worthy of the faith of its prophets.*
>
> **— General Carl A. 'Tooey' Spaatz,**
> ***Evolution of Air Power*, Military Review, 1947**

ROLE OF AIR, SPACE, AND CYBERSPACE POWER IN SA

The role of air, space, and cyberspace capabilities in SA is founded on the characteristics of air and space resources. These characteristics (range, speed, precision, flexibility and lethality) enable a JFC to access to the depths of adversary's centers of gravity where land and maritime forces cannot easily reach. Added to traditional domains is the cyberspace domain. Employing the Air Force's cyber capabilities throughout this domain, in combination with the traditional capabilities of air and space power, allows synergy and flexibility across a range of lethal and non-lethal options. Air, space, and cyber power used in SA comprises the JFC's maneuver elements that can operate in the third dimension. Through cyber power, the commander has access to the cognitive and information dimensions that can give an asymmetric advantage and unprecedented access to an adversary's decision-making cycle. Through the employment of Air Force forces and capabilities, the JFC is not limited to two-dimensional warfare, using his surface forces in a series of tactical battles to position maneuver elements that threaten an adversary's centers of gravity. The application of airpower, integrated with information operations, creates effects more rapidly than surface forces alone, thereby accessing the psychological and cognitive aspects of warfare directly. Properly employed, SA is the Air Force's most decisive warfighting capability.

STRATEGIC ATTACK IN IRREGULAR WARFARE OPERATIONS

Throughout history, strategic attack has been employed as part of traditional warfare between states and groups of states for "traditional" military purposes—political victory in the context of those nation states' purposes. Strategic attack has a place in irregular warfare (IW)—violent struggle among state and non-state actors for legitimacy and influence over the relevant population—as well. The COG in IW is generally the relevant populace and the intent of warfare conducted in this realm is to favorably influence the COG, not "attack" it. Airpower can influence this strategic COG positively and directly in many different ways; these are detailed in AFDD 2-3, Irregular Warfare. There are uses for strategic attack in IW which have historically shown wide applicability:

- Conducting precision-strike operations that eliminate enemy personnel, resources, and infrastructure while minimizing unintended collateral on innocent members of the populace—all of which enhances the legitimacy and effectiveness of the supported government, reassures the populace, and undermines popular support for the enemy. The killing of al Qaeda leader Abu Musab al-Zarqawi in June of 2006 is an example of this.

- Conducting precision cyberspace strikes on enemy financial resources to deny use of these resources, as has been done throughout OEF and OIF.

- Conducting strikes or raids on enemy weapons of mass destruction caches or production facilities, to prevent use of these weapons as part of enemy strategy, as in striking chlorine storage facilities in Iraq to prevent this chemical WMD from being used in insurgent improvised explosive devises.

CHAPTER TWO

COMMAND AND CONTROL

Order or disorder depends on organization.

— **Sun Tzu**

Effective command and control arrangements and relationships are crucial to the success of SA. **Unity of effort is key to the success of SA operations and can only be achieved through command and control arrangements that ensure unity of command.** The COMAFFOR/joint force air and space component commander (JFACC) should be the supported commander for SA operations who, in turn, supports the achievement of the JFC's objectives. The concept of centralized control and decentralized execution of air and space forces is vital to effective SA because the synergy of all applied force elements is needed to debilitate the adversary's willingness and capability to wage war. The fragmented air command structure used during the Vietnam War proved that piecemeal application of force by the various Air Force and other Service force elements dilutes the effectiveness of an operation and often serves to extend an operation without achieving US national or military objectives.

CENTRALIZED CONTROL AND DECENTRALIZED EXECUTION

Two tenets of air and space power that drive the discussion of how to achieve unity of command for air forces are flexibility and versatility. They are also keys to ensuring unity of effort of a strategic air campaign. Flexibility allows power to be applied to multiple missions and tasks often with little, if any, weapons or systems modifications. Even with this inherent flexibility, however, there is rarely enough airpower available to satisfy all demands. The versatility is derived from the fact that it can be employed to achieve effects at the strategic, operational, and tactical levels of warfare. Centralized control of resources maximizes airpower's potential by emphasizing the integration of limited air, space, and cyber resources during planning for operations. It also minimizes undue dissipation and fragmentation of effort and ensures coherence and focus on essential national or theater objectives. Because no single commander can personally direct all the detailed actions of a typical complement of forces, decentralized execution of missions and tasks is usually necessary and is accomplished by delegating appropriate authority for execution. As a rule, centralized control of operations ensures effective employment of limited assets, while decentralized execution allows tactical adaptation and accommodates the components' different employment concepts and procedures in a joint environment.

However, the nature of SA operations may require increased direct influence in execution. Centralized control, to focus the effective capabilities against desired tasks, and decentralized execution, to give tactical commanders the ability to fight in the most effective way, continue to be the preferred methods to employ air, space, and cyberspace power. SA operations, however, may require very precise timing and highly focused actions based upon rapidly changing intelligence. In these circumstances, increased direct influence into tactical-level execution of SA missions may be appropriate. Nevertheless, centralized control and decentralized execution remain fundamental tenets of air, space, and cyberspace power employment. Commanders should continue to push decision-making authority to the lowest practical and appropriate level.

The combined air and space operations center (CAOC) integrates all air and space operations into a seamless whole based on the JFC's guidance.

COMMAND RELATIONSHIPS

SA is employed in a joint construct in a unified command structure under the authority of combatant commanders tasked at the direction of the President and Secretary of Defense (SecDef). In this context, air, space, and cyber forces organize, train, equip, and plan as an integral element of a joint or multinational force. However, the air component can be employed independently of the surface components in a joint force to help a JFC achieve objectives. This is particularly true for operations with strategic objectives that require direct attack. The criteria to attack using the air component independent of surface components of the joint force depend on the expected effectiveness and availability of capabilities appropriate to achieving the desired effects. In most instances, deep-ranging Air Force forces would be employed in conjunction with other component air elements of the joint force.

The command relations described in Joint Publication (JP) 1, *Joint Warfare of the Armed Forces of the United States* and AFDD 2 apply when conducting SA. If air, space, and cyber forces comprise the preponderance of SA capability, the JFACC should be the supported commander for SA operations. In other instances, the JFC/combatant commander may wish to retain direct control of SA operations in order to integrate and coordinate the efforts of all participating components and agencies.

US Strategic Command (USSTRATCOM) creates global attack plans (both nuclear and non-nuclear) based on guidance from the President and SecDef and designates appropriate assets to achieve desired effects. Under these circumstances, the combatant commander (theater or USSTRATCOM) may opt to form a single-

Service task force. This task force would maintain a C2 system designed to quickly disseminate posturing and execution orders from the President and SecDef to the forces in the field. During operations in support of a geographic combatant commander, USSTRATCOM will coordinate strikes with the affected combatant commander. However, USSTRATCOM may relinquish operational control (OPCON) or tactical control (TACON) of these forces to the supported commander if directed by the President or SecDef.

Some assets critical to effective SA may operate from other combatant commanders' areas of responsibility (AORs). OPCON of strategic attack assets operating from CONUS or stationed in another AOR outside the theater of operations, may transfer to the supported JFC. For instance, in Operation IRAQI FREEDOM, B-2s launching from CONUS and B-52s launching from Europe were employed in US Central Command's AOR. These forces were attached with specification of OPCON to Commander, US Central Command who, in turn, delegated OPCON to Commander, US Central Command Air Forces. Circumstances may require other arrangements, but these arrangements should be worked out as far in advance and in as much detail as possible to avoid confusion. See AFDD 2 for more specific guidance on command relationships.

Special operations forces (SOF) offer a unique set of capabilities that may be leveraged to support SA. SOF may conduct SA unilaterally, or in conjunction with other forces, but they normally do not fall under the operational control of the air and space component. SOF air assets may require air component support to conduct their missions and in some instances SOF ground personnel may require air component close air support or air interdiction. They may also enable other components to perform SA through special reconnaissance or other actions. As an example, during Operation DESERT STORM, SOF directed coalition aircraft to targets as part of SCUD-hunting efforts. During OEF and OIF, similar operations were conducted to target Taliban, al Qaeda, and Iraqi leadership.

When air operations constitute the bulk of SA capability, the JFC will normally task the JFACC, as a supported commander, to conduct such operations. Acting in this capacity, the JFACC can assess the effects required, define the objectives to be achieved, designate targets to be attacked, integrate air operations and allocate air and space resources to achieve the desired effects and objectives. Centralized control and decentralized execution maximizes the synergy between SA and other uses of military power in achieving national or theater objectives.

CHAPTER THREE

PLANNING AND ASSESSMENT

When blows are planned, whoever contrives them with the greatest appreciation of their consequences will have a great advantage.

— Frederick the Great

SA should be a key element of any warfighting strategy. It has been a major element of every conflict the United States has engaged in since World War II and has enhanced or decisively shaped many of them. This powerful weapon in the JFC's arsenal cannot be employed effectively if it is not well understood. At the tactical level— to aviators in the cockpit—SA missions look very much like any other force application mission, and this may incline strategists at the operational level to treat them as such. However, there are significant differences between SA and counterforce missions, especially in terms of planning and assessment.

Planning and assessment are combined in this chapter because many of the considerations that govern the former apply to the latter as well. As part of an effects-based approach, they form a seamless whole with employment (covered in Chapter 4) in the context of an overall strategy. Planning before operations will obviously be separated in time from employment and assessment, but many of the factors that guide them are the same and should be considered during planning. Once an operation's battle rhythm has begun, the three operate together as part of an ongoing cycle.

PLANNING

SA in Campaign Planning

SA planning requires understanding not only of the strategic level of warfare, where the effects of SA are manifested, but also of the operational level of war, because it is at this level the planning, conduct, control, and sustainment of SA occur. Hence, planning should take place within the overall context of campaign planning.

The COMAFFOR should provide the JFC with SA options early in the planning process. Even though SA is a function often carried out by Air Force forces, it is vital that its use be sponsored and embraced at the JFC/combatant commander level during course of action (COA) development and before component planning starts and before COAs are developed. To be used effectively, SA should be integrated and sequenced with other instruments of national power. For example, some forms of coercive diplomacy may require that political actions be carefully synchronized with military actions in order to credibly convey a threat of force or an appropriate sense of urgency. SA during LINEBACKER II in Vietnam was carefully orchestrated with diplomatic overtures to North Vietnam, the Soviet Union, and China, which combined to coerce a peace settlement with terms acceptable to the US. Other situations may require the careful integration of informational or economic efforts as well.

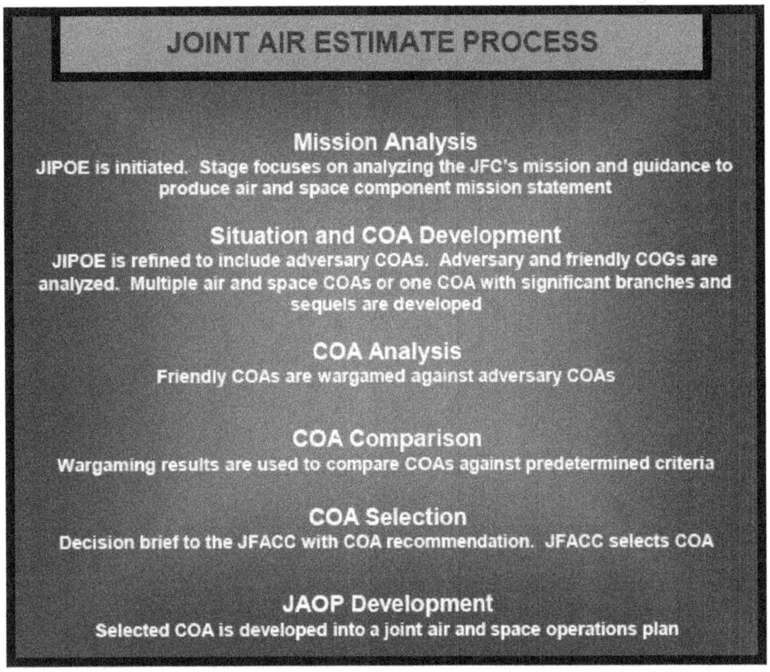

Figure 3.1. The Joint Air Estimate Process
[Based on JP 3-30, *Command and Control for Joint Air Operations*]

Once planning for an operation is initiated, the JFC's strategic estimate constitutes the "first look" at military objectives, the strategic environment, the threat, and possible alternative COAs. This is when a COA featuring SA, whether stand-alone or in a complementary role, should be introduced. The COMAFFOR, as the component commander possessing the preponderance of capability, should recommend a SA option at this stage even though taskings to the components have not yet been formalized.

Analysis usually contained in the strategic estimate can be vital for effective SA operations. The estimate should include an evaluation of enemy leadership (in particular its underlying psychology and motivations), governing mechanisms, bureaucratic politics, and political vulnerabilities. Enemy leadership is usually the "target audience" (if not the outright target) for SA and so it is vital to understand how the leadership thinks, gathers/disseminates information and what underlies its choice of COAs. The estimate may also be the only place where strategic COGs, the focus of SA, are defined. Analysis of leadership in the estimate is critical because some aspect of the leadership most often comprises a strategic COG. Even if leadership is not the sole COG, its connectivity and relationship to others shape how other COGs are affected. Proper strategic-level causal linkage analysis is a critical part of strategic attack planning.

SA in Air Operations Planning

Planners formulate COAs for the COMAFFOR to recommend to the JFC through the joint air and space estimate process (JAEP), which is the air component portion of the joint operations planning process. The JAEP culminates in production of the joint air and space operations plan (JAOP), which details how air and space efforts will accomplish or support the JFC's overall objectives. The JAEP consists of the following stages: mission analysis, situation and COA development, COA analysis, COA comparison, COA selection, and JAOP development. The following discussion highlights considerations specific to planning SA within the JAEP.

Mission Analysis

The mission analysis portion of the JAEP establishes the purpose of the operation and broad guidance for its conduct, usually expressed in terms of a JFACC's mission statement. This stage is also where joint intelligence preparation of the operational environment (JIPOE) begins. A thorough understanding of the adversary, the adversary's centers of gravity and critical infrastructure and support mechanisms is critical. Thoroughly understanding when, where, and how to attack the adversary's military targets is essential to achieving military objectives. Further, understanding the historical, cultural and economic sensitivities is critical for justifying the use of force and gaining the support (or at least the acquiescence) of the target audience. Figure 3.1 illustrates the JAEP.

Objectives and Intent. Determining the purpose of the operation and its desired outcome—establishing the objectives and end state—is the most important part of mission analysis. **Effective use of SA requires clear, attainable, relevant, and decisive objectives. It also requires clear definition of the commander's criteria for the operation's overall success—a logical and achievable end state.**

Clear understanding of the commander's intent, which consists of the end state, objectives, and a comprehensive method for accomplishing them, is especially critical for SA operations. This is greater than for many other forms of force application, which primarily engage enemy fielded forces. Most counterforce applications seek to achieve strategic objectives through accumulation of tactical- and operational-level effects against enemy fielded forces. Since the defeat of fielded forces will usually aid achievement of strategic-level objectives, efforts against these forces may still be of value even if strategic objectives are not clearly developed. This is not so with SA. Unclear or unattainable objectives will lead to ineffective operations. This is especially so when SA is used in concert with other instruments of national power such as diplomacy. Objectives that were unclear and unattainable within the context of North Vietnamese motivations (e.g., "create conditions for a favorable settlement by demonstrating to the North Vietnamese that the odds are against their winning") contributed to failure of the SA portion of Operation ROLLING THUNDER in Vietnam. Even though closely coordinated with diplomatic efforts, the 1966-67 bombing accomplished no effects that contributed to attainment of national objectives and sent confusing signals to the enemy, the enemy's allies, and the rest of the world, and emboldened the North Vietnamese to expand their involvement in the insurgent struggle in South Vietnam.

Joint Intelligence Preparation of the Operational Environment. Successful SA operations place unique demands on intelligence professionals involved in planning them. "Traditional" intelligence methods are well suited to estimating the strength and disposition of enemy forces. Even the intent of the enemy's military forces can usually be surmised from their overt actions. As planning progresses, the effects of force-on-force engagement are relatively easy to estimate, since cause and effect relationships are generally straightforward and well understood, and measures of effect (MOEs) are easy to derive, especially if attrition-based.

This is not the case with SA, which requires clear and in-depth understanding of two vital areas beyond those traditionally focused on during JIPOE. The first is how the enemy functions as a system—how the various components of their state, group, or entity interact and support one another; which functions are key to sustaining other functions; what processes are required to keep the system running; and so on. Those components or processes that enable many other components of the system to function are often the most lucrative targets, as transportation and oil were during the strategic bombing campaign of World War II. Enemy leadership is always such a component and, by definition, is always in some way a target of SA.

The second vital JIPOE requirement is to understand the causal linkages between actions and effects. As stated before, the effects of SA are almost always indirect—there is some intervening mechanism (often there are several) between the direct effects of attack and the ultimate outcome. This means that some thought must be put into determining these mechanisms or causal linkages—in thinking through the likely consequences of attacks beyond the immediate damage caused by the bombs (or missiles, SOF actions, cyber actions (such as computer network attack, etc.).

> *Defeat of the enemy consists in overcoming the resistance concentrated in his center of gravity....*
>
> **— Carl von Clausewitz, *On War***

Deriving such intelligence and analyzing it properly are not easy tasks. In-theater intelligence and assessment resources are geared to give limited target systems analyses, but are probably not sufficient for the kind of in-depth understanding necessary for successful SA. Planners can obtain assistance from organizations outside the theater (like the Joint Warfare Analysis Center (JWAC)) or outside the DOD (like the Central Intelligence Agency), and may even require insight from intelligence assets of foreign governments. These agencies should know what is required of them and working relationships should be built before operations begin. In many cases appropriate access will require coordination above the JFC level.

Situation and Course of Action Development

Situation Development. This phase of planning begins with a crucial refinement of the ongoing JIPOE process. Compelling an enemy to do our will requires denying them those things they need to continue the fight or placing at risk those things they value—we must critically weaken their sources of power. Thus we must understand what their sources of power are and where those sources are, or can be made, critically vulnerable and where decisive points for attack are. This may be accomplished through COG analysis.

Center of Gravity Analysis. A center of gravity is a source of power that provides moral strength, freedom of action, or will to act. In the context of SA against enemy systems (nation, alliance, or other group), COGs are focal points that hold a system or structure together and draw power from a variety of sources and provide purpose and direction to that system. In practical terms COGs can be thought of as balance points, focal points, or leverage points that, if have appropriate action taken against them, will have a greater affect on the overall system that has been targeted. They provide a means of relating critical system elements to those that are vulnerable—determining critical vulnerabilities. Critical vulnerabilities will have decisive points within them; attacking these will critically affect the COG and confer decisive advantage for friendly commanders.

COGs differ from operation to operation. In the case of a major campaign against an industrialized opponent, the adversary's war sustaining resources may constitute a COG and its critical vulnerability may be the transportation system that serves all of its elements. Decisive points may be nodes within that system. This was the case in World War II in Europe, for instance. In the case of stability operations, the leadership of an adversary terrorist network may be the COG and the means of affecting it may be cyber-operations based SA against its means of financial support, which may have decisive points vulnerable to cyber attack. Some aspect of the adversary's leadership will likely form a COG regardless of the type of conflict, even though the means of affecting it may change from situation to situation.

Affecting the appropriate COGs in the right way should have the most decisive effect on a conflict. A number of tools and models exist to aid planners in analyzing COGs and how to best attack them. Regardless of the analysis method used, opportunities exist to achieve physical and coercive effects that are well out of proportion to the effort and resources required to accomplish the attacks. Identifying these opportunities requires sophisticated analysis of a specific system's COGs which gives a broad view of those parts of the enemy's system that friendly action should orient upon.

One of the key insights of the systems approach is that it emphasizes the vulnerability of complex systems to attacks upon the linkages and interrelationships among components. In many cases, it may be beneficial to strike at a COG through parallel attack. This may synergistically place greater stress on the COG than sequential or serial attack could alone. Allied attacks against the German rail network accomplished this effect during the last ten months of World War II. Allied bombers struck rail yards, while near-parallel attacks by medium altitude bombers and fighters destroyed rolling stock and rail track away from cities. These efforts crippled a system the Germans relied upon for freedom of action.

Another technique involves affecting target systems so as to expose new, more accessible vulnerabilities. During Operation DESERT STORM, coalition forces disabled a key portion of the fiber optic network in the Iraqi communication system in order to force reliance on more exploitable forms, such as ultrahigh frequency radios.

Course of Action Development, Analysis, Comparison, and Selection

Subsequent phases of the JAEP involve the development, analysis, comparison, and selection of COAs. COAs address who, what, when, where, how, and why joint air operations are to be conducted, including objectives, forces required, and concepts for projecting, employing, and sustaining those forces. In many cases SA will form part of a larger COA or set of COAs, complementing efforts against fielded forces and action by nonmilitary elements of national power, as it did in both Europe and the Pacific in World War II and again in OIF. In some cases, it may form a distinct phase, "sub-campaign," or sequel within a larger conflict, as LINEBACKER II did in Vietnam or the bombing of Serbia did in OAF. In other cases, it may be employed in an independent COA, an alternative to force-on-force engagement. Finally, SAs may be employed separately to accomplish very specific purposes, as in Doolittle's raid on Tokyo, US and British strikes on Rome in 1943 (helping bring about Italian surrender), or Israel's attack on Iraq's Osiraq nuclear reactor in 1981. Regardless of how large or small a part of the joint campaign, however, planners should develop and validate a concept of operations for SA, just as they do for counterforce applications.

When developing COAs, planners should think through the causal links between an affected system or target and the achievement of objectives. This is not easy—it is much more art than science. These links almost always involve subjective judgments about the nature of the enemy and how they will react to us, especially at the very highest levels of the "causal chain," where changes in actual behavior occur. Ultimately, COA development should discern objectives, tasks, measures, and indicators to create effects among adversary systems in a manner consistent with the operation's assumptions, guiding strategy, and end state. In doing so, the campaign transitions from merely dismantling the systems studied in the COG analysis phase to creating appropriate effects at the right time in the proper location. Sorting out the linkages will probably require assistance from sources outside the theater and insight from sources with deep knowledge of the enemy. Automated tools may someday help sort through them, but such tools will only be as accurate as the underlying assumptions planners make concerning enemy motivations, psychology, and structure.

Wargaming. Planners should be aware that during the COA analysis and comparison phases of the JAEP, it may be difficult to accurately wargame the effects of SA.

Counterforce operations (e.g., counterland) are somewhat easier to model, since the effects of attrition on enemy forces are often assumed to be linear. The effects of SAs are most often nonlinear and simple force-on-force models are not useful in predicting outcomes. This is true even of strikes against enemy resources, due to the complex adaptive nature of economic activity. It is essential that COA comparison and wargaming be done qualitatively, not just quantitatively, and airmen should be prepared to speak to the complex, nonlinear nature of effects on enemy leadership, perceptions, strategies, and systems. A wargaming format that emphasizes friendly action, enemy reaction, and friendly counteraction may be best suited for SA planning.

The unsuccessful Allied SA effort against the German ball bearing industry during their bombing effort offers an excellent illustration of difficulties involved in determining and modeling (or wargaming) causal linkages. Operations analysis revealed that ball bearings represented a critical potential bottleneck in the German war economy. Virtually all German manufactured machinery used them, and over half of all used were manufactured at a single plant in Schweinfurt. In 1943, US bombers leveled the plant, reducing German ball bearing production by 38% in one strike. Unfortunately for the Allies, the Germans had anticipated such an attack and had laid up months of reserve stock, purchased tons more from neutral nations, begun the full-scale dispersal of the industry, and researched use of a different type of bearing that was more readily available. The Schweinfurt raid, though successful in its direct effects, ultimately failed to have the desired effect on the Nazi war effort. Even the opportunity costs involved in dispersing the industry and researching use of alternative bearings represented net improvements for the German war economy. Further, the price Germany exacted for the raid (over 15% losses) forced Allied planners to dramatically reduce attacks on German industry until a greater degree of air superiority could be attained.

Branches and Sequels. The Schweinfurt raid points out another element critical to successful SA planning and COA selection: The anticipation of likely enemy responses to our actions. Planners and commanders should assume the enemy is intelligent and adaptive; that he will develop ways to work around the damage caused to his systems, or find ways to deny elements of friendly strategy (especially easy to do when subjected to serial attacks). We should anticipate those workarounds and build branches and sequels into our plans accordingly.

Branches are options built into the basic or initial plan. They will usually have a specific trigger or triggers delineated, such as a particular enemy action or success of a friendly operation. In terms of SA, a branch might involve shifting the COG or COGs the friendly effort is focused upon, opening or closing certain target systems to attack, escalating or de-escalating the intensity of effort. In 1943, senior Allied leaders built the option to bomb Rome into plans for the invasion of Italy. Implementation of this branch had the desired effects, hastening the downfall of the Mussolini government and Italian surrender.

A branch may also entail a change in the way force is applied through SA. LINEBACKER II represented a dramatic increase in the tempo and intensity of SA coupled with a change in target focus, as did the last several weeks of operations during OAF. Both efforts were successful. Such branches should be planned before operations begin.

Sequels are subsequent operations based on possible outcomes of current operations. At the operational level, campaign phases can be viewed as sequels to the basic plan. They usually represent larger changes in focus or emphasis than branches do. The strategic bombing campaign against Germany involved several sequels—in this case implicit campaign phase changes—as the Germans devised workarounds to the damage caused by Allied bombing. The largest was a shift in early 1944 away from bombing war-sustaining resources for their own sake to bombing aircraft production infrastructure and Berlin, which had the effect of drawing the Luftwaffe into the teeth of escorting Allied fighters. SA became subordinate to a larger offensive counterair effort until the Luftwaffe was defeated. Essentially, this shift represented a new phase of the Allied bombing effort. "Industrial web" bombing resumed in full force (and was much more effective) after defeat of the Luftwaffe, introducing another phase or sequel. Of course, "reactive phasing" is not the best way to conduct operations. Sequels in the form of phases should be planned for and made part of the JAOP.

Joint Air Operations Plan Development

Air component planning culminates in production and validation of a JAOP, which provides general guidance and a framework for succeeding air operations directives, master air attack plans, air tasking orders, and similar products that direct air and space efforts once execution has begun. There are a number of considerations unique to SA operations that planners should consider as they assemble the JAOP.

Targeting Considerations. As the JAOP is developed, commanders and planners should continually assess whether the military effects they are planning to impose are achievable and support the campaign's overall objectives. As planning progresses into tactical tasks and individual targets, planners sometimes have a tendency to devolve into "input" or "target-based" planning rather than effects-based planning. Planners may begin to say, "The plan has these resources; what can we hit with them?" or "let's hit the usual list of targets," rather than determining the desired effects on the enemy system and then deriving resources and capabilities required to achieve those effects. Input-based planning often leads to logical disconnects between ends and means, such as military COAs that cannot achieve the overall political goals, as was the case in Vietnam. Such logical disconnects may not seriously hamper efforts to defeat enemy fielded forces. However, such disconnects may greatly hamper SA efforts, because success usually requires clear understanding of the more complex logical links between actions and desired effects. The temptation to resort to an inputs-based approach often becomes more pronounced as planning progresses into execution and the stress of a daily battle rhythm. Planners should be aware of this temptation and compensate. Commanders should be prepared to redirect or refocus planners if they see this happening. Airmen should think effects-based if they are to successfully operate effects-based.

Force Considerations. Airmen should be aware that a wide variety of tools can perform SA operations. There is no such thing as an inherently "tactical" or "strategic" asset—virtually any system, regardless of what it is ordinarily used for, may contribute to the overall SA effort. Planners should think broadly: many options will be available. They should avoid resorting to a particular system or weapon because "that's what we usually use." The desired effects should drive the capabilities used and the targets selected.

ASSESSMENT

The conceptual problems in constructing an adequate or useful measure of military power have not yet been faced. Defining an adequate measure looks hard, and making the estimates in real situations looks even harder.

— Andrew W. Marshall

Assessment is essential to successful operations in general and successful SA in particular. It is integral to the effects-based planning-execution-assessment cycle from beginning to end. Planning for it should begin long before forces are engaged and actual assessment efforts may continue long after a conflict ends. It informs day-to-day operations once a battle rhythm is established and influences doctrine, strategy, and even procurement in peacetime. Analysts involved in the assessment process are a vital part of US warfighting efforts. Operational and campaign assessment, performed by the air component and JFC respectively, extend analysis far beyond the tactical realm of combat assessment and are especially vital to SA efforts. The focus of these must go beyond assessments of battle damage or weapons effectiveness to anticipatory judgments about what effects SA may have over the course of a campaign or a conflict.

Nonetheless, assessment is often the most difficult part of the planning-employment-assessment cycle to perform consistently well. While direct physical effects normally provide key indicators for measuring the success or effectiveness of an operation, the indirect effects are most important for the SA effort and are harder to measure, relying on qualitative and subjective measures of effectiveness, not quantitative and empirical measures of performance. This will continue to present significant challenges to analysts for the foreseeable future.

Planning for Assessment

The industrial measures [the US Strategic Bombing Survey] utilized to criticize the Combined Bomber Offensive (CBO) [were] simply too coarse and unappreciative of all but the most direct economic and military effects of strategic bombing.

— **James G. Roche and Barry D. Watts,**
Choosing Analytic Measures

Planners, commanders, and analysts may not know the impact of SAs immediately because SA most often works through psychological, systemic, cascading, or other higher-order effects. Therefore, successful SA may depend on anticipatory operational and campaign assessment done as part of planning. Accurate assessment provides the groundwork for analysts to determine how well the plan is developing during execution. This applies even more so to SA operations. The subjective and sometimes tenuous linkage between cause and effect could make intermediate steps in the effects chain hard to detect, leading to the false impression that particular operations are ineffective. As with JIPOE, deriving such insight is not easy and should be thoroughly planned for. Planners will need help from national-level assets (many of the same used for "up-front" analysis) and since these resources are "low density, high demand," gaining access will be much easier if coordinated early. Planners and intelligence collection managers should also consider ongoing collection requirements during plan execution: What type of information will be needed, what assets will be needed, and how will these assets be controlled and sustained. Planners should be as thorough and detailed when planning for assessment as when planning for any other aspect of SA.

Requirements

SA is able to impose systemic/functional and psychological effects that may achieve strategic objectives more directly than defeat of enemy fielded forces. Historically, the ability to measure such effects in order to gauge effectiveness (overall progress toward objectives) has been very limited. Traditional assessment efforts were geared to analyzing the immediate, physical effects of combat: The attrition of enemy troops or equipment, or the damage to facilities caused directly by bombs or other weapons. Planners and analysts during World War II, Vietnam, and even Operation DESERT STORM lacked tools with which to evaluate their progress. Even the US Strategic Bombing Survey (USSBS) after World War II, as deep and comprehensive an analysis as has ever been done, relied on very simplistic linear measures to gauge economic effects of the Allied bombing effort, ignoring much beyond direct production figures. This missed many of the indirect effects—military, economic, political, and psychological—such as the diversion of resources to air defense and the growing popular pressure for retaliation that led the Nazi regime to waste resources on largely ineffective terror weapons like the V-1 and V-2.

In general, strategists need to know what kind of indicators can be used to determine progress toward achievement of particular effects and objectives. Most of the indicators available are objective and quantitative; they help measure physical effects. What is often most important for SA operations are subjective and qualitative indicators that help measure indirect effects, especially in realms like economic and psychological impact. These will most likely have to be derived by planners themselves, or by the analysts and intelligence managers assisting them. Some easily quantifiable measures exist, but they may often be deceiving (like the USSBS' production figures). Planners may be tempted to use them because they are easy to obtain, but should understand their limitations. Some qualitative measures may be straightforward; if enemy capitulation is the objective, it either happens or it doesn't. Most will be much less "black or white," involving a range or gradation of possible effects that will be hard to measure objectively. The indirect economic effects of Allied bombing during World War II are examples. So are the beneficial effects friendly actions have upon parties outside a conflict, like the influence NATO attacks on Serbia had in getting the Russians to coax Milosevic to concede during OAF. Nonetheless, these are real effects that may have a great deal more influence upon strategy and the conduct of operations than do more easily quantifiable effects.

Progress toward accomplishment of even straightforward objectives like surrender can often be very difficult to measure. In many cases, complex systems accumulate effects over time that move them toward a change in state or behavior, but may not exhibit indicators of change until a critical point is reached, at which time the system will fail catastrophically. The point at which this "catastrophe" will occur is often impossible to predict reliably. This was the case with the final deterioration of the German war economy in early 1945, the sudden and unexpected collapse of the Soviet Union in 1991, and the rapid collapse of the Taliban regime in Afghanistan during OEF. This unpredictability may frustrate strategists and leaders as a conflict progresses and may translate into pressure to change COAs, refocus efforts, or divert resources from SA prematurely.

Operational Assessment (OA) and Campaign Assessment

Planners, in conjunction with intelligence and operations research analysts, should develop solid and logical measures and indicators, and plan for ways to collect intelligence against them during execution. From the Air Force perspective, this effort is the responsibility of the operational assessment team within the strategy division of the AOC. OA evaluates the performance of the commander's air and space strategy in terms of its ability to achieve desired effects and objectives. It builds on the objective analysis performed during combat assessment, taking a critical look at the selected strategy and COAs to determine if adjustments need to be made. OA is the "entering argument" for assessment of SA, but is only a starting point. Deriving the necessary measures and collection requirements is difficult, conceptually and practically, and commanders should not restrict the assessment to component efforts. Campaign analysis at the JFC level will add perspective, as will assistance from organizations like JWAC and other national-level resources. Assistance from such organizations should be planned for and coordinated as early as possible.

CHAPTER FOUR

EMPLOYMENT CONSIDERATIONS

RESOURCES

SA may be carried out with nuclear and conventional global strike capabilities from all the components: bombers, attack aircraft, SOF, ballistic and cruise missiles, information operations, offensive space capabilities, and surface forces. Each system or weapon has unique capabilities that should be exploited based on the nature of the desired effects. Normally, Air Force forces will have the preponderance of capability to conduct and support SA operations.

CHEMICAL, BIOLOGICAL, RADIOLOGICAL, AND NUCLEAR (CBRN) WEAPONS CONSIDERATIONS

Nuclear operations are a form of SA, authorized only by the President of the United States, which can produce political and psychological effects well beyond their actual physical effects. The employment of nuclear weapons may lead to such unintended consequences as escalation of a current conflict or long-term deterioration of relations with other countries. For this reason above all others, the decision whether or not to use, or even threaten to use, nuclear weapons will always be a political decision, not a military one.

The fundamental purpose of US nuclear forces is deterrence and in that context, the US uses nuclear weapons every day. Deterrence attempts to dissuade or prevent an adversary's, or potential adversary's, leadership from initiating a course of action contrary to our interests. An adversary must believe the cost of aggression against the US, its interests, or its allies will be so high as to outweigh any possible gain. Thus, deterrence attempts to maintain the status quo while ultimately influencing the state of mind in the adversary's leadership to a point where the course of action is not even contemplated. Deterrence requires the US to maintain the ability to use force and the credible threat of the use of that force. Without the capability and perceived will to use nuclear weapons, deterrence will fail.

It is stated US policy not to employ biological or chemical weapons. CBRN weapons have great potential for any foe who seeks to induce strategic effects. For example, such weapons may be used to induce terror or mass dislocation, to deter a course of action (e.g., intervention), to deny access, to blackmail, or to enhance international prestige. Air and space forces should be prepared to deter CBRN use and respond against any adversary that threatens to use or uses CBRN. Preemptive SA against an adversary's CBRN capability before it can be weaponized, relocated, exported, hidden, or used may be a commander's best option against those threats. The growing danger from proliferation of such weapons requires that air and space forces be capable of locating and attacking them with a high degree of accuracy, in order to ensure their destruction while minimizing collateral damage.

The potential for catastrophic collateral damage is a particularly important concern when attacking such weapons directly. If an enemy relocates CBRN weapons systems close to civilian population centers with the intent of shielding them from attack (a violation of Article 58 of Additional Protocol 1 of the Geneva Conventions), it may be politically, legally, or morally difficult to target them unless their use is certain and imminent. In such cases, an indirect approach may be better. Directly attacking production or supporting infrastructure, such as plants where nontoxic chemical precursors are made or key means of transportation used to move them may have the desired effects and achieve the objectives. It may be necessary to use nonlethal means to force an adversary to move the weapons to locations where they can be safely attacked. It may also be safest to degrade or destroy some production facilities before they begin production, as the Israelis did against Iraq's Osiraq nuclear reactor in 1981. Close coordination of SA with information and diplomatic efforts are especially important when preemptive strikes against CBRN capabilities are considered, since strategies to publicly justify the strikes or mitigate the undesired effects of collateral damage are likely to play a central role in both deterring the adversary and sustaining political will for subsequent attacks. Targeting decisions against potential CBRN threats involve significant issues under the law of war and should be assessed for compliance with international law, including the law of armed conflict, and relevant US treaty obligations.

During the Cuban Missile Crisis [and] the Korean War...the possibility of nuclear use—by one side—contributed to successful coercive diplomacy. As the confrontation over Cuba unfolded, US intelligence informed the Kennedy administration that Soviet nuclear forces were in a poor state of preparedness and that the United States could, if necessary, launch a devastating first strike with a low probability of a robust Soviet response. This dominance allowed Kennedy to stake out a demanding public profile; he knew that the costs of escalation would weigh more heavily on Moscow. In the Korean War, the North agreed to accept talks leading to the continued partition of the country in part because of the election of President Eisenhower, who threatened the use of nuclear weapons to end the conflict.

—Daniel Byman, Matthew Waxman, and Eric Larson,

Air Power as a Coercive Instrument

ELEMENTS OF EFFECTIVE EMPLOYMENT

Parallel versus Sequential Operations

SA is normally most effective when employed using parallel operations. Strikes on COGs are almost always necessary, but a parallel approach—simultaneously striking a wide array of targets chosen to cause maximum shock effect across an enemy system—limits an adversary's ability to adapt and react and thus places the most stress on the system as a whole. This may offer the best opportunity to trigger system-wide shock, thus inducing paralysis or collapse. The object is to effectively control the opponent's strategic activity through rapid decisive operations. Even when this is not fully realized, parallel attack should work synergistically with other actions to cause favorable changes in enemy behavior.

> *The successful prosecution of parallel war requires more than compressing sequential attacks into one simultaneous attack. Parallel war exploits three dimensions—time, space, and levels of war. In the opening hours of the Gulf War, all three dimensions were exploited:*
>
>
> - *Time—within the first 90 minutes over 50 separate targets were on the master attack plan. Within the first 24 hours, over 150 separate targets were designated for attack.*
> - *Space—the entire breadth and depth of Iraq was subjected to attack. No system critical to the enemy escaped targeting because of distance.*
> - *Levels of war—national leadership facilities (strategic level), Iraqi air defense and Army operation centers (operational level), and Iraqi deployed fighting units—air, land, and sea (tactical level)—came under attack simultaneously.*
>
> **—Maj Gen David A. Deptula,**
>
> ***Effects-based Operations: Change in the Nature of Warfare***

Examples of successful parallel attack at the operational level abound. Coalition forces effectively destroyed Iraqi ground resistance using this approach during Operation DESERT STORM and OIF. The Israelis used similar methods to achieve similar results against Arab armies in the 1956 and 1967 wars, and the Egyptians achieved it at the tactical level against the Israeli Bar-Lev defensive line in 1973. While the theoretical ideal of complete paralysis was not achieved in any of these instances, enemy forces were still prevented from functioning as coherent systems through the mechanism of parallel attack. SA aims at similar effects upon an enemy system as a whole. The Allies sought such effects against Germany during World War II's allied bombing effort, enjoying success during the last ten months of the war in Europe, when near-parallel and unrelenting attack on Germany's transportation network became feasible on a large scale. Coalition bombing during Operation DESERT STORM also approached this result, but the effect was fleeting and did not prevent the Iraqis from taking action such as launching the SCUD campaign against Israel. Similar bombing in OIF may have been more effective if it worked synergistically with parallel attacks against Iraqi fielded forces to ensure swift victory. While not foolproof, a parallel approach may hold the best prospect of causing cascading changes throughout an enemy system.

In some circumstances, parallel operations may not be possible or desirable. Typically, political or resource constraints are what preclude the use of parallel operations. In these cases, attacks should be conducted so that the resulting effects attain the objectives in priority order. When employed this way, much of the mass and shock effect of air and space power may be compromised.

One of the highest-priority enabling objectives for air commanders will always be to gain the degree of air superiority needed to make other operations possible. Developments in air defense technology may necessitate devoting a substantial weight of effort to obtaining air superiority. The employment of stealth assets may reduce the weight of effort required. This should be done in concert with (and sometimes before) SA operations are commenced if there is a significant risk of losing the assets employed. The US found this was necessary during World War II, having lost thousands of bombers in attacks against the heart of Europe before switching focus to defeat of the Luftwaffe in early 1944. The effectiveness of Allied bombing improved remarkably after this was accomplished. The Israelis also found it necessary to neutralize the Egyptian ground-based air defense system before their air force could operate effectively during the 1973 Yom Kippur War.

It is possible to combine parallel and sequential attack strategies. Such a combination recognizes those cases where constraints and restraints may limit the ability to carry out simultaneous attacks, but incorporates as many of the advantages of parallel attack as possible. In combined parallel and sequential operations, high priority objectives are the focus of the initial air and space effort. At phase points, the campaign can be expanded to incorporate additional objectives, while continuing to ensure the previous requirements are met. For example, the first air and space objectives might be to isolate national leadership; destroy CBRN and the means of delivery; achieve air, space, and information superiority; and destroy certain C2 capabilities. Once these objectives have been met, air and space operations could then expand to incorporate additional objectives, such as disruption of national fuel stocks, electric power, and transportation systems, or dislocation of enemy fielded forces. In effect, this was the approach adopted in Operation DESERT STORM, although the first "phases" were completed much faster than originally planned. The JFACC can tailor a campaign in this manner to a level that maximizes intensity but maintains focus and enhances control. A phased strategy, with varying operational intensity, may also be forced on commanders by external constraints, as occurred in OAF.

Coercion

Coercion is a concerted effort to modify an adversary's behavior by manipulating the actual or perceived costs and benefits of continuing or refusing to pursue a certain course of action. A coercive strategy may involve one or more of several potentially overlapping mechanisms to include denial, decapitation, power base erosion, unrest and weakening.

The mechanism by which SA can most effectively coerce the enemy is through denial whereby it threatens the enemy with defeat or prevents it from achieving its military objectives. In this way, denial seeks to change enemy behavior by hindering or destroying his capability to fight. Denial can be implemented in two ways; counter-force or counter-strategy. Counter-force reduces the enemy's capability to carry out its intended actions by affecting its ability to fight while counter-strategy seeks to convince the enemy that its actions will not succeed, instilling a sense of hopelessness. Denial convinces the enemy that defeat is inevitable and that it would be more prudent to capitulate sooner rather than later. In other cases, denial induces strategic paralysis within entire enemy systems, thus rendering effective resistance impossible, i.e., denying the enemy the ability to act at least temporarily. The Allied bombing effort and Pacific bombing campaigns that targeted German and Japanese industrial resources and the coalition strategic air effort against the Iraqi regime during Operation DESERT STORM and OIF are examples of denial.

Decapitation threatens the enemy's military and national leadership. Attacking the military chain of command via counter-control decapitation supports denial by rendering enemy command and control ineffective. Attacking national leadership via counter-regime decapitation supports power base erosion by putting at risk the regime's ability to maintain power. Enemy regimes either comply with the coercer's demands or risk removal from power.

Power base erosion is tied to decapitation and involves threatening a regime's relationship with its key supporters. SA can accomplish this by using air strikes to turn elites against a regime or foster concern among key decision-makers. This mechanism can backfire, however. For example, in Operation El Dorado Canyon, US air strikes on Moammar Qhaddafi's command center, a naval special operations training school, a military portion of the Tripoli airport, and barracks of elite troops did not have one of their intended effects—provoking the Libyan military to overthrow his regime. Instead, the raids appeared to strengthen Qaddafi vis-à-vis his rivals.

Finally, SA of valid military objectives can have the coercive effect of creating unrest among an enemy's population and/or weakening of the enemy's infrastructure. These mechanisms are aimed at impacting the enemy's popular will or perception. In the past, these mechanisms have involved directly targeting civilian populations to increase disaffection and pressure the adversary leadership to accept the demands of the coercer. However, the legality and morality of directly attacking an enemy's civilian populace is against international law concerning the conduct of war. The US remains committed to these laws and principles that support them. Additionally, historical evidence suggests that strategies directed against an enemy's population seldom succeed. Now, however, with the advent of precision weaponry, the US is capable of carefully regulating the destructive effects of SA thereby minimizing collateral damage. This capability enables the US to use these coercive mechanisms in a way that complies with the laws of armed conflict.

Early attempts to coerce the enemy through SA had a mixed record of success. In the Korean War, the "strategic" air effort against the North's resources was unsuccessful, however, North Korean concerns that we would escalate by using nuclear weapons helped bring about a permanent cease-fire. Initial SA efforts in Vietnam also failed due to a fundamental misunderstanding of the nature and motivation of the enemy. Nevertheless, LINEBACKER II did aid in persuading the North Vietnamese to accept a limited settlement that permitted US withdrawal from the war. The advent of precision weaponry and stealth, however, enables a more discriminate use of airpower, improving SA's coercive ability. In fact, coercive use of SA proved indispensable to success in ODF and OAF.

Past operations have shown that successful coercion with air and space power is a product of one or more of the following factors:

Escalation Dominance. Escalation dominance is the ability to increase the enemy's costs of defiance while denying them the opportunity to neutralize those costs or counter-escalate. Nuclear retaliation remains the ultimate form of escalation dominance and its threat is still valuable in deterring an adversary's use of CBRN, but many non-nuclear applications of SA offer options as well. The credible threat of a major increase in the tempo or destructiveness of bombing may be effective, as may a change in intended effects: Switching from attacks on purely military targets to attacks on dual-use infrastructure (civilian infrastructure supporting military functions). Both of these proved effective during OAF. Escalation dominance should be planned through the full spectrum of actions and counter-actions in the conflict. Effective use requires a clear understanding of the desired friendly political and military end state.

Defeating the Enemy's Strategy. SA can accomplish this in a variety of ways. One of the most obvious, deterring or denying use of CBRN, may be accomplished through threat of nuclear retaliation or by limited or threatened conventional attacks on production and delivery systems. Direct strikes against enemy leadership (as in OEF), or its connectivity to instruments of national power (such as control links to fielded forces, as in Operation DESERT STORM), can remove strategic options. Effects of the latter sort may be difficult to achieve with SA alone, however.

Magnifying Threats from Third Parties. In many cases, threats to a hostile regime from third-party sources, such as internal dissidents or a nation external to the conflict, can wield significant coercive power. SA can contribute to such coercive efforts by reducing the ability of an adversary to defend against a hostile third power or by weakening internal control mechanisms, thus highlighting the fragility of the regime. Efforts of the latter sort played a part in Saddam Hussein's decision to begin his troops' withdrawal from Kuwait during Operation DESERT STORM, and in Slobodan

Milsoevic's decision to come to terms with NATO during OAF. Strikes against dual-use assets like electrical power, in addition to having system-wide denial effects, may prove effective in coercing regimes in which popular unrest is an issue.

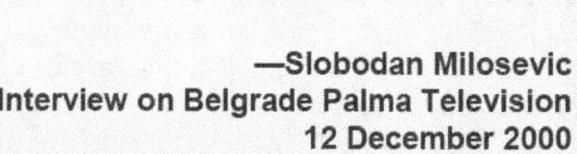

> *I think...that had we [the Serbian government] rejected that joint [peace] proposal of...the G-7 plus Russia, then there would have been yet another change for the worse that would have placed yet another trump card into the hands of our enemies.... Without doubt, even more massive bombing would have followed in retaliation, with the loss of a great number of lives.*
>
> **—Slobodan Milosevic**
> **Interview on Belgrade Palma Television**
> **12 December 2000**

Credible Threat or Use of Force. The use of SA, or the threat of its use, should be credible in an adversary's mind if coercion is to be successful. Through words and actions, we must be able to convey to the enemy that we can and will deliver on our promises. Success hinges on the integration of physical attacks with the right informational, diplomatic or economic activities to demonstrate that we have both the will and the capability to endanger what they value. The restricted and graduated nature of US SA efforts in Operation ROLLING THUNDER failed to convey to the North Vietnamese leadership that we intended to inflict damage meaningful enough to warrant even a temporary halt to their military action in South Vietnam. In LINEBACKER II, by contrast, the US was able to deliver a threat of retaliation with sufficient scope and intensity to coerce a limited settlement from North Vietnam.

There is a danger here: While successful threats or use of force can enhance credibility, unsuccessful use can as easily destroy credibility. The "mystique" of certain forms of airpower (such as the B-52 bomber) helped convey the seriousness of US intent during the LINEBACKER operations. On the other hand, some have argued that airpower "failed" in Vietnam, hurting America's overall military credibility. While US failure in Vietnam was a failure of overall political and military policy, not of airpower alone, the perception of the "failure of airpower" in some circles led many to discount its capabilities as a coercive tool for a number of years. This may have contributed to Saddam Hussein's decision calculus when planning for Iraq's invasion of Kuwait in 1990 (Hussein's pre-war statements concerning US airpower lend credence to this idea) and contributed to the failure of American efforts to coerce Iraqi withdrawal from that country during Operation DESERT SHIELD.

Enemy Vulnerability and Susceptibility to Coercion. Not all enemies can be coerced and an enemy who was successfully coerced in the past may not be coercible in the future. For coercion to succeed, the enemy must not be so desperate or so devoted to their course of action that they are unwilling to change their behavior for anything short of complete subjugation. Traditionally, parties to ethnic, religious, civil, or national liberation wars have been difficult to coerce. Coercion may still be possible in such conflicts, but it may be more difficult, take more time, and require more force to affect. In general, the coercive "track record" of SA in Vietnam was very poor, due mainly to the implacability of enemy leadership. A dramatic escalation in the level of force used, however, did wring moderate concessions from the North Vietnamese during LINEBACKER II, albeit at a substantial political cost back in the US.

Detailed Understanding of Enemy Leaders' Thinking and Motivations. This is necessary for most aspects of planning and executing SA, but is particularly vital for successful coercion. US failure to understand North Vietnamese leadership led to coercion's poor performance in that war. Much more sophisticated appreciation of the enemy (for example, strike and information operations against dual-use commercial assets controlled by the Serbian ruling elite) enabled successful coercion of Slobodan Milosevic during OAF.

Complementary Operations and Synergy

While SA offers commanders independent, potentially decisive options, it is usually most effective when employed in conjunction with surface forces and other instruments of national power. SA contributes to and benefits from the synergistic effects of other operations. Counterspace and information operations separate an adversary from indigenous or third party support, preventing enemy space or information systems from interfering with SA. Surface maneuver benefits from and supports SA by creating a dynamic environment that the enemy must confront with degraded capabilities. Land offensives create high demands upon both enemy infrastructure and fielded forces by speeding consumption of vital war materiel, thus potentially creating enemy critical vulnerabilities.

SA may have immediate effects that enhance other operations. For example, during Operation DESERT STORM, one objective was to sever Iraqi leadership's communication links to its fielded forces. The critical vulnerabilities within these links were the fiber optic lines that ran across the Tigris River bridges in Baghdad. Coalition aircraft destroyed these bridges, crippling the Iraqi national C2 network, which greatly contributed to accomplishment of theater objectives against Iraqi forces in addition to weakening Iraqi leadership.

Complementary operations can enhance delayed strategic effects. Many times, counterforce operations can work hand-in-hand with SA to place maximum pressure on an enemy system. Similarly, SA can be used to force crucial elements of enemy fielded forces into a conflict, where they can be destroyed by complementary counterforce action.

During the CBO, the Allies waged an extended strategic attack campaign against German oil production before the effects became apparent. German oil consumption began to exceed production in May 1944 and by December the fuel shortage reached catastrophic proportions. The Germans launched the Battle of the Bulge in December 1944 in part to capture Allied stocks of fuel, but failed when many Panzer units ran out of fuel before reaching their objectives. Strategic attack and counterair efforts also worked synergistically to help defeat the Luftwaffe in early 1944, by offering the Germans bomber formation targets they couldn't ignore in order to draw German fighters into the teeth of the new US P-47 and P-51 fighter escorts. Germany's pilots, not its airframes, were its vulnerability. The result took months, but was decisive in achieving the Allies' counterair objectives.

"Between January and April 1944 our daytime fighters lost over 1,000 pilots. They included our best squadron, Gruppe and Geschwader commanders. Each incursion of the enemy is costing us some fifty aircrews. The time has come when our weapon is in sight of collapse."

—General der Jagdflieger Adolf Galland
Luftwaffe War Diaries

PITFALLS AND LIMITATIONS

SA has a proven record of success, but it has also failed in application in a number of cases. Failure was generally due to poor understanding of the enemy or of the pitfalls inherent in a conceptually difficult form of force application. Success requires careful planning; thorough, sophisticated understanding of the enemy; complete knowledge of one's own capabilities, requirements, and vulnerabilities; and anticipation of the effects that problems like friction, incrementalism, misprioritization, and restraints/constraints can have on operations.

Friction

The workings of chance and the natural inertia that exist within any large organization, like a military force, play havoc in all forms of warfare. There are, however, elements of Clausewitz's concept of "friction" that uniquely influence very complex operations like SA. These include, but are not limited to:

Imperfect Knowledge and Misunderstanding. All forms of warfare may suffer from imperfect understanding of the enemy and their motivations, but SA will almost certainly fail if the enemy is seriously misjudged. Such was the case in Vietnam, where both the military and civilian authorities misunderstood the nature of the conflict and the enemy's degree of resolve. This resulted in part from "mirror-imaging," assuming that the enemy's motivations and priorities are similar to our own. Planners and commanders can guard against the dangers inherent in imperfect knowledge (but not eliminate them entirely) by trying to understand the conflict from the enemy's perspective.

A "Target Servicing" or Attritional Mindset. One of the sources of friction inherent in much US warfighting has been the devolution of effects-based planning and execution into a simplistic approach focused on attrition of enemy systems or the servicing of target lists. This occurs because the latter approach is conceptually simpler and is easier to implement in practice. If enemy fielded forces are the focus of the air and space effort, such a mindset may not significantly hamper operations, even though it is fundamentally a less efficient way to approach warfighting. In SA operations, however, such an approach is almost always harmful. A robust effects-based approach to warfighting, enforced by commanders, is the best means to avoid a shift to target-servicing or attrition.

Unintended Direct Effects—Collateral Damage. US forces will always be directed to minimize civilian casualties and mitigate collateral damage. First, America's moral values demand it. Second, the US is committed to adhering to the Geneva Conventions and other international laws and customs pertaining to the way we conduct war and armed conflict. Third, the goodwill of populations in countries whose ruling regimes we are fighting is often an important element in US strategy and this will be harmed by such damage. When it does occur, it may significantly hamper operations, usually by making commanders or national leaders more cautious.

This happened following the coalition bombing of the al Firdos C2 bunker in Baghdad during Operation DESERT STORM. As a major national military command center, this was a legitimate and legal target for SA, but the unfortunate fact that the attack killed many civilians the Iraqi regime had quartered in its top levels harmed US efforts publicly and hampered strikes on targets near the center of Baghdad for the rest of the war.

Also, while the US must fight to win, collateral damage may complicate reconstruction and stability operations efforts and diminish popular support for military operations, thus directly hampering attainment of the overall end state. Careful planning, especially for intelligence collection and strategic communication requirements, and precise crafting of rules of engagement can mitigate some of the dangers of unintended consequences and collateral damage, but cannot eliminate them entirely.

Unintended Indirect Effects. The cause and effect chain is usually very complex in SA operations and some actions will almost certainly entail consequences that cannot be foreseen. These consequences can be good or bad from the friendly perspective, but some will inevitably hurt friendly efforts. An example of both followed in the wake of the Doolittle Raid: Many indirect results of the raid were favorable and helped shorten the war, but the raid also provoked the Japanese into a major retaliatory campaign in eastern China that cost the Allies tens of thousands of casualties.

"Kill Chain" Considerations. A form of friction inherent in the way US forces are organized and controlled may affect the prosecution of time-sensitive or fleeting strategic targets. Striking such targets will likely have high-level political implications and therefore may require approval from the JFC or even the President. The unique political nature of SA may, of necessity, add layers and seams to the target approval process, which costs the executing commander time. Successful strikes, however, may require swift action. This essential tension has led to the escape of important fleeting targets in the past. Modern communication technology has made it possible to compress the time required to find, fix, track, target, and engage such targets, but has not compressed decision time involved in attacking them. In fact, it may even lengthen the time required to obtain approval to attack politically sensitive targets. Effective operations against such targets require careful planning beforehand and thorough understanding of the risks and consequences of ad hoc SA without careful prior coordination at all levels of command, and a shared view of the intent of commanders above the JFACC's level.

Failure of Analysis

Sometimes the intelligence preparation process is simply wrong in choosing COGs or their critical vulnerabilities. Among the more famous examples is the case of early operations analysts choosing the German ball bearing industry as a focus for attack. Assuming a static, unreactive enemy is most often the cause of such analysis failures. Strategists must never lose sight of the fact that the enemy is a thinking, adaptive agent and that war is fundamentally a contest of wills. Wargaming friendly COAs against the gamut of potential enemy COAs, a process built into the joint planning construct, is the best way to avoid such failures, but no method is foolproof. Planners should expect that the enemy will aggressively attempt to defeat US SA efforts by continually adapting its defensive strategies.

For success, two major problems must be solved—dislocation and exploitation…. The importance of these two problems has never been adequately recognized—a fact that goes far to explain the common indecisiveness of warfare.

—B.H. Liddell Hart

History has shown that one of the most powerful methods of defeating an enemy is to impose shock upon them. In many cases, the most efficient use of SA is to impose shock directly upon enemy leadership or upon an entire enemy system at the strategic level. Such a strategy may not be appropriate for all conflicts. Nonetheless, in those cases where it is possible and appropriate, there may be pressure on commanders to employ force incrementally or sequentially, in ways that prevent the imposition of system-wide shock and dislocation ("gradualism"). This may arise from a lack of understanding of the nature of armed conflict on the part of higher-level leadership (as was the case with President Johnson and SecDef McNamara during Vietnam). It may also arise if the military personnel prosecuting a conflict devolve into a "target-servicing" or attritional mindset. The first problem may be intractable from the COMAFFOR's perspective (although commanders should make the effort to convince those "up the chain" of the correct course of action), but the second can be combated with thorough planning and conscious maintenance of an effects-based approach throughout a conflict.

Technical or physical limitations may also force incremental or sequential operations, as the limitations of existing weapon systems did during World War II and Vietnam. Lack of available resources may do so as well. Planners and commanders must be flexible and adaptive, always prepared to seek the highest "payoff" for the least "cost" in operations. The increasing sophistication of the planning tools used for SA may help ameliorate some of these considerations.

Misprioritization

The prioritization of SA missions versus others may create dilemmas for the JFACC as well as the JFC. Air and space power is immensely flexible and capable and will always be pulled in different directions by competing demands. Since SA represents the highest potential payoff, commanders should avoid the temptation to divert resources from it to service the operational- or tactical-level fight, unless it is necessary in the JFC's view to affect. Near-term parts of the fight may be more urgent, but they are not necessarily more important. The temptation to divert resources may be exacerbated by the fact that it is sometimes difficult to perceive progress toward SA's objectives until they are met. As a general rule, SA should constitute a campaign's highest priority unless the JFC deems other efforts essential for attainment of campaign objectives or survival of some part of the joint force is threatened.

Restraints and Constraints

Commanders operate within political, legal, and diplomatic restraints and constraints that may force less than optimal uses of military power and should consider them during planning and employment. Restraints prohibit certain actions; constraints compel them. Commanders should realize that political considerations may limit or meter the pace of a campaign, and may even dictate incremental or sequential air operations. During OAF, an early gradualistic approach to the campaign was a political necessity until consensus developed among NATO allies that stronger military force would be necessary to prevail. Some research suggests that this benefited the NATO effort by affording escalation dominance. In other cases, however, restrictions may hamper even combined SA/diplomatic efforts and prevent effective coercion, as happened during ROLLING THUNDER.

In conducting SA, commanders are constrained under the law of war by their obligation to minimize enemy civilian casualties. Their need to minimize friendly combatant casualties is another necessary constraint. Additionally, commanders are restrained from striking targets of special cultural, religious, or humanitarian significance, especially because they generally have no value as targets in the enemy's system. Commanders are constrained to minimize friendly combatant and enemy civilian casualties. Restraint and constraint challenges include:

* Proactively articulating how SA operations can achieve the combatant commander's objectives for the existing political and diplomatic situation. It may help to point out that SA often offers the least expensive alternative in terms of physical destruction.

* Monitoring the political and diplomatic situation to anticipate events and circumstances that affect SA operations.

* Developing and implementing proactive strategic communication operations to establish and maintain the credibility and legitimacy of SA options within the information environment.

* Developing alternative plan branches and sequels based on probable changes in the political and diplomatic environment.

Failure of Assessment

Assessment failures can degrade effectiveness, cause unnecessary expenditure of resources, or even cause SA operations to fail. Such problems most often result from a lack of assessment planning. In Operation DESERT STORM, almost no assessment planning was done and all echelons in the process lacked trained personnel and other resources. As a result, many important targets, like WMD storage facilities and electrical system components, were struck again and again, long after initial precision strikes had destroyed them. While this did not cause operations to fail, it did divert scarce resources from other priorities and place flyers at risk over well-defended targets. Robust assessment and intelligence, surveillance and reconnaissance collection planning are the best preventive measures.

CONCLUSION

The proper use of air, space, and cyber superiority, centralized command and control, and accurate intelligence assessment are vital to successful SA. Realizing that SA can be the most effective use of limited Air Force forces, commanders should be willing to resist the temptation to divert resources to other efforts unless such diversions are vital to attaining objectives or to the survival of an element of the joint force. Whether used in parallel attack that overwhelms enemy systems with multiple crises or more limited strikes that disrupt or coerce the enemy, SA can have a decisive impact in war and its aftermath.

At the very heart of warfare lies doctrine...

SUGGESTED READINGS

Air Force Publications (Note: All Air Force doctrine documents are available on the Air Force Doctrine Center web page at https://www.doctrine.af.mil)

AFDD 1, *Air Force Basic Doctrine*

AFDD 2, *Operations and Organization*

AFDD 2-1, *Air Warfare*

Joint Publications

JP 1, *Doctrine Warfare of the Armed Forces of the United States*

JP 3-0, *Joint Operations*

JP 3-12, *Doctrine for Joint Nuclear Operations*

JP 3-30, *Command and Control for Joint Air Operations*

JP 5-0, *Joint Operations Planning*

DOD Publications

DOD Directive 5100.1, *Functions of the Department of Defense and its Major Components.*

Other Publications

Alberts, David S. and Czerwinski, Thomas J., eds., *Complexity, Global Politics, and National Security* (Washington DC: National Defense University). 1997.

Barlow, Jason B., *Strategic Paralysis: An Airpower Theory for the Present* (Maxwell AFB AL: Air University Press). 1994.

Daniel Byman and Matthew Waxman, *The Dynamics Of Coercion : American Foreign Policy And The Limits Of Military Might* (Cambridge ; New York : Cambridge University Press). 2002.

Byman, Daniel L., Matthew C. Waxman and Eric Larson, *Air Power as a Coercive Instrument* (Santa Monica, CA: RAND). 1999.

Davis, Richard G., *Decisive Force: Strategic Bombing in the Gulf War* (Washington, DC: Air Force History and Museums Program). 1996.

Deptula, David A., *Effects-Based Operations: Change in the Nature of Warfare* (Arlington: Aerospace Education Foundation). 2001.

Fadok, David S., *John Boyd and John Warden: Air Power's Quest for Strategic Paralysis* (Maxwell AFB, AL: Air University Press). 1995.

Felker, Edward J., *Airpower, Chaos, and Infrastructure: Lords of the Rings* (Washington DC: National Defense University). 1998.

Hinman, Ellwood P., *The Politics of Coercion: Toward a Theory of Coercive Airpower for Post-Cold War Conflict* (Maxwell AFB, AL: Air University Press). 2002.

Hosmer, Stephen T., *Operations Against Enemy Leaders* (Santa Monica, CA: RAND). 2001

Hosmer, Stephen T., *The Conflict Over Kosovo: Why Milosevic Decided to Settle When He Did* (Santa Monica, CA: RAND). 2001.

Keaney, Thomas A. and Eliot Cohen, *Revolution in Warfare: Air Power in the Persian Gulf* (Annapolis: Naval Institute Press). 1995.

Keaney, Thomas A. and Eliot Cohen, *Gulf War Air Power Survey Summary Report* (Washington DC: US Government Printing Office). 1993.

Lambeth, Benjamin S., *The Transformation of American Air Power* (Ithaca, NY: Cornell University Press). 2000.

Liddell Hart, B. H., *Strategy* (New York, Praeger). 1967.

Mann, Edward C.; Gary Endersby; and Thomas R. Searle; *Thinking Effects: Effects-Based Methodology for Joint Operations* (Maxwell AFB, AL: Air University Press). 2002.

Pape, Robert A., *Bombing to Win: Air Power and Coercion in War*, (Ithaca NY, Cornell University Press). 1996.

Roche, James G. and Barry D. Watts, "Choosing Analytic Measures," *Journal of Strategic Studies* 11, issue 2, pages 165-209. 1991.

Strange, Joe, *Centers of Gravity and Critical Vulnerabilities: Building on the Clausewitzian Foundation So that We Can All Speak the Same Language* (Quantico, VA: Marine Corps University). 1996.

Schelling, Thomas C., *Arms and Influence* (New Haven CT, Yale University Press). 1966

Schelling, Thomas C., *The Strategy of Conflict* (Boston MA, Harvard University Press). 1970

Strange, Joe. *Capital "W" War* (Quantico, VA: Marine Corps University). 1998.

The United States Strategic Bombing Surveys (European War, Pacific War Summary Volumes) (Maxwell AFB, AL: reprinted by Air University Press). 1987.

Warden, John A., III. *The Air Campaign: Planning for Combat* (Washington, DC: National Defense University Press). 1988.

Warden, John A., III. "The Enemy as a System," *Air Power Journal*, Spring 1995

Watts, Barry D., et al, *Gulf War Air Power Survey, Vol II, Part II, Effects and Effectiveness* (Washington, DC: US Government Printing Office). 1993.

Watts, Barry D., *Clausewitzian Friction and Future War*, (Washington, DC: National Defense University Press). 1996.

GLOSSARY

Abbreviations and Acronyms

AFDD	Air Force doctrine document
AOC	air and space operations center [USAF]
AOR	area of responsibility
C2	command and control
CAOC	combined air and space operations center
CBO	combined bomber offensive (World War II)
CBRN	chemical, biological, radiological, and nuclear
CFACC	combined force air and space component commander
COA	course of action
COG	center of gravity
COMAFFOR	commander, Air Force forces
CONUS	continental United States
DOD	Department of Defense
IADS	integrated air defense system
JAEP	joint air and space estimate process
JAOC	joint air and space operations center
JAOP	joint air and space operations plan
JFACC	joint force air and space component commander
JFC	joint force commander
JIPOE	Joint intelligence preparation of the operational environment
JP	joint publication
MOE	measures of effectiveness
NATO	North Atlantic Treaty Organization
OA	operational assessment
OAF	Operation ALLIED FORCE
OEF	Operation ENDURING FREEDOM
ODF	Operation DELIBERATE FORCE
OIF	Operation IRAQI FREEDOM
OPCON	operational control

RAF	Royal Air Force (UK)
SA	strategic attack
SCUD	surface-to-surface missile system
SecDef	Secretary of Defense
SOF	special operations forces
TACON	tactical control
USAF	United States Air Force
USSBS	United States Strategic Bombing Survey
USSTRATCOM	United States Strategic Command
WMD	weapons of mass destruction

Definitions

air and space power. The synergistic application of air, space, and information systems to project global strategic military power. (AFDD 1)

air interdiction. Air operations conducted to destroy, neutralize, or delay the enemy's military potential before it can be brought to bear effectively against friendly forces at such distance from friendly forces that detailed integration of each air mission with the fire and movement of friendly forces is not required. Also call **AI**. (JP 1–02)

assessment. Analysis of the security, effectiveness, and potential of an existing or planned intelligence activity. (JP 1-02). [*The evaluation of progress toward creation of effects and the achievement of objectives and end state conditions.*] {Italicized words in brackets apply only to the Air Force and are offered for clarity.} (AFDD 2)

campaign. A series of related military operations aimed at accomplishing a strategic or operational objective within a given time and space. (JP 1–02)

campaign plan. A plan for a series of related military operations aimed at accomplishing a strategic or operational objective within a given time and space. (JP 1–02)

cascading effect. One or more of a series of successive indirect effects that propagate through a system or systems. Typically, cascading effects flow throughout the levels of conflict and are the results of interdependencies and links among multiple connected systems. (AFDD 2)

causal linkage. An explanation of why an action or effect will cause or contribute to a given effect. It answers the question, "why do planners believe this action will create or help create the desired effect?" (AFDD 2)

center of gravity. The source of power that provides moral or physical strength, freedom of action, or will to act. Also called **COG**. (JP 5.0 SD) [*In the context of strategic attack against enemy systems, COGs are focal points that hold a system or structure together and draw power from a variety of sources and provide purpose and direction to that system.*] {Italicized definition in brackets applies only to the Air Force and is offered for clarity.} (AFDD 2-1.2)

centralized control. 1. In air defense, the control mode whereby a higher echelon makes direct target assignments to fire units. 2. In joint air operations, placing within one commander the responsibility and authority for planning, directing, and coordinating a military operation or group/category of operations. (JP 1-02) [*The planning, direction, prioritization, allocation, synchronization, integration, and deconfliction of air and space capabilities to achieve the objectives of the joint force commander.*] {Italicized definition in brackets applies only to the Air Force and is offered for clarity.} (AFDD 1)

combatant command. A unified or specified command with a broad continuing mission under a single commander established and so designated by the President, through the Secretary of Defense and with the advice and assistance of the Chairman of the Joint Chiefs of Staff. Combatant commands typically have geographic or functional responsibilities. (JP 1-02)

command and control. The exercise of authority and direction by a properly designated commander over assigned and attached forces in the accomplishment of the mission. Command and control functions are performed through an arrangement of personnel, equipment, communications, facilities, and procedures employed by a commander in planning, directing, coordinating, and controlling forces and operations in the accomplishment of the mission. Also called **C2**. (JP 0-2)

counterspace. Those offensive and defensive operations conducted by air, land, sea, space, special operations, and information forces with the objective of gaining and maintaining control of activities conducted in or through the space environment. (AFDD 2-2)

critical vulnerability. An aspect or component of a critical requirement, which is deficient or vulnerable to direct or indirect attack that will create decisive or significant effects. (Upon approval of JP 5.0, this term and its definition and will be included in JP 1-02.) (JP 5.0 FD)

cyberspace. The notional environment in which digitized information is communicated over computer networks. (JP 1-02). [*A domain characterized by the use of electronics and the electromagnetic spectrum to store, modify and exchange data via networked systems and associated physical infrastructure.* (AFDD 1)] {Text in brackets applies only to the Air Force and is offered for clarity.}

decentralized execution. Delegation of execution authority to subordinate commanders. (JP 1-02) [Decentralized execution of air and space power is the delegation of execution authority to responsible and capable lower-level commanders to achieve effective span of control and to foster disciplined initiative, situational responsiveness, and tactical flexibility.] {Italicized definition in brackets applies only to the Air Force and is offered for clarity.} (AFDD 1)

decisive point. A geographic place, specific key event, critical factor, or function that, when acted upon, allows commanders to gain a marked advantage over an adversary or contribute materially to achieving success. (This term and its definition are provided for information and are proposed for inclusion in the next edition of JP 1-02 by JP 3-0.)

direct effect. First order result of action with no intervening effect or mechanism between act and outcome. Usually immediate, physical, and readily recognizable (e.g., weapons employment results). (AFDD 2)

effects. A full range of outcomes, events, or consequences of a particular cause. The cause may be an action, a set of actions, or another effect. The action can derive from any element of power—economic, political, military, diplomatic, or informational—and may occur at any point across the continuum from peace to global conflict. (AFDD 2-1.2)

effects-based. Actions, such as operations, targeting, or strategy that are designed to produce distinctive and desired effects while avoiding unintended or undesired effects. (AFDD 2-1.2)

effects-based approach to operations. An approach in which operations are planned, executed, assessed, and adapted to influence or change systems or capabilities in order to achieve desired outcomes. (AFDD 2-1.2)

indirect effect. A second, third, or nth-order effect created through an intermediate effect or causal linkage following a causal action. It may be physical, psychological, functional, or systemic in nature. It may be created in a cumulative, cascading, sequential, or parallel manner. An indirect effect is often delayed and typically is more difficult to recognize and assess than a direct effect. (AFDD 2)

information operations. The integrated employment of the core capabilities of electronic warfare, computer network operations, psychological operations, military deception, and operations security, in concert with specified supporting and related capabilities, to influence, disrupt, corrupt or usurp adversarial human and automated decision making while protecting our own. Also called IO. (JP 1-02)

joint force air component commander. The commander within a unified command, subordinate unified command, or joint task force responsible to the establishing commander for making recommendations on the proper employment of assigned, attached, and/or made available for tasking air forces; planning and coordinating air operations; or accomplishing such operational missions as may be assigned. The joint force air component commander is given the authority necessary to accomplish missions and tasks assigned by the establishing commander. Also called **JFACC**. (JP 1-02). [*The joint force air and space component commander (JFACC) uses the joint air and space operations center to command and control the integrated air and space effort to meet joint force commander's objectives. The Air Force position is that air power and space power together create effects that cannot be achieved through air or space power alone.*] {Italicized words in brackets apply only to the Air Force and are offered for clarity.} [AFDD 2]

joint force commander. A general term applied to a combatant commander, subunified commander, or joint task force commander authorized to exercise combatant command (command authority) or operational control over a joint force. Also called **JFC**. (JP 1–02)

maneuver. 1. A movement to place ships, aircraft, or land forces in a position of advantage over the enemy. 2. A tactical exercise carried out at sea, in the air, on the ground, or on a map in imitation of war. 3. The operation of a ship, aircraft, or vehicle, to cause it to perform desired movements. 4. Employment of forces in the battlespace through movement in combination with fires to achieve a position of advantage in respect to the enemy in order to accomplish the mission. (JP 1–02)

measures of effectiveness. Tools used to measure results achieved in the overall mission and execution of assigned tasks. Measures of effectiveness are a prerequisite to the performance of combat assessment. Also called **MOEs.** (JP 1-02)

operational control. Command authority that may be exercised by commanders at any echelon at or below the level of combatant command. Operational control is inherent in combatant command (command authority) and may be delegated within the command. When forces are transferred between combatant commands, the command relationship the gaining commander will exercise (and the losing commander will relinquish) over these forces must be specified by the Secretary of Defense. Operational control is the authority to perform those functions of command over subordinate forces involving organizing and employing commands and forces, assigning tasks, designating objectives, and giving authoritative direction necessary to accomplish the mission. Operational control includes authoritative direction over all aspects of military operations and joint training necessary to accomplish missions assigned to the command. Operational control should be exercised through the commanders of subordinate organizations. Normally this authority is exercised through subordinate joint force commanders and Service and/or functional component commanders. Operational control normally provides full authority to organize commands and forces and to employ those forces as the commander in operational control considers necessary to accomplish assigned missions; it does not, in and of itself, include authoritative direction for logistics or matters of administration, discipline, internal organization, or unit training. Also called **OPCON.** (JP1-02)

operational level of war. The level of war at which campaigns and major operations are planned, conducted, and sustained to accomplish strategic objectives within theaters or other operational areas. Activities at this level link tactics and strategy by establishing operational objectives needed to accomplish the strategic objectives, sequencing events to achieve the operational objectives, initiating actions, and applying resources to bring about and sustain these events. These activities imply a broader dimension of time or space than do tactics; they ensure the logistic and administrative support of tactical forces, and provide the means by which tactical successes are exploited to achieve strategic objectives. (JP 1–02)

psychological operations. Planned operations to convey selected information and indicators to foreign audiences to influence their emotions, motives, objective reasoning, and ultimately the behavior of foreign governments, organizations, groups, and individuals. The purpose of psychological operations is to induce or reinforce foreign attitudes and behavior favorable to the originator's objectives. Also called **PSYOP**. (JP 1–02)

strategic air warfare. Air combat and supporting operations designed to effect, through the systematic application of force to a selected series of vital targets, the progressive destruction and disintegration of the enemy's war-making capacity to a point where the enemy no longer retains the ability or will to wage war. Vital targets may include key manufacturing systems, sources of raw material, critical material, stockpiles, power systems, transportation systems, communication facilities, concentration of uncommitted elements of enemy armed forces, key agricultural areas, and other such target systems. (JP 1–02)

strategic attack. Strategic attack is offensive action that is specifically selected to achieve national or military strategic objectives. These attacks seek to weaken the adversary's ability or will to engage in conflict, and may achieve strategic objectives without necessarily having to achieve operational objectives as a precondition. Also called **SA**. (AFDD 2-1.2)

strategic communication. Focused United States government (USG) efforts to understand and engage key audiences in order to create, strengthen or preserve conditions favorable for the advancement of USG interests, policies, and objectives through the use of coordinated programs, plans, themes, messages, and products synchronized with the actions of all elements of national power. (JP 1-02)

strategic level of war. The level of war at which a nation, often as a member of a group of nations, determines national or multinational (alliance or coalition) security objectives and guidance, and develops and uses national resources to accomplish these objectives. Activities at this level establish national and multinational military objectives; sequence initiatives; define limits and assess risks for the use of military and other instruments of national power; develop global plans or theater war plans to achieve these objectives; and provide military forces and other capabilities in accordance with strategic plans. (JP 1–02)

tactical control. Command authority over assigned or attached forces or commands, or military capability or forces made available for tasking, that is limited to the detailed direction and control of movements or maneuvers within the operational area necessary to accomplish missions or tasks assigned. Tactical control is inherent in operational control. Tactical control may be delegated to, and exercised at any level at or below the level of combatant command. When forces are transferred between combatant commands, the command relationship the gaining commander will exercise (and the losing commander will relinquish) over these forces must be specified by the Secretary of Defense. Tactical control provides sufficient authority for controlling and directing the application of force or tactical use of combat support assets within the assigned mission or task. Also called **TACON**. (JP 1–02)

tactical level of war. The level of war at which battles and engagements are planned and executed to accomplish military objectives assigned to tactical units or task forces. Activities at this level focus on the ordered arrangement and maneuver of combat elements in relation to each other and to the enemy to achieve combat objectives. (JP 1–02)